GOOD SEX

A Couple's Guide

Contains adult content

Nicci Talbot

Good Sex – A Couple's Guide is also available in accessible formats for people with any degree of visual impairment. The large print edition and eBook (with accessibility features enabled) are available from Need2Know. Please let us know if there are any special features you require and we will do our best to accommodate your needs.

First published in Great Britain in 2012 by
Need2Know
Remus House
Coltsfoot Drive
Peterborough
PE2 9BF
Telephone 01733 898103
Fax 01733 313524
www.need2knowbooks.co.uk

Contents

Introduction

Type 'how to have good sex' into Google and there are (at the time of writing) 75,500,000 global monthly searches. Related search terms include 'orgasm', 'how to satisfy a woman in bed', 'sex positions for pregnancy', 'anal sex', 'vitamins to boost sex drive', 'tips for good phone sex', 'good sex small penis', 'good lubricants for sex', 'good places to have sex', and so on.

Sex is one of life's pleasures, but for many of us it's also a source of anxiety. Am I vocal enough? Are we having enough sex? Where has my libido gone? Feeling anxious about sex and relationships is normal; we all have these concerns and we should let them go says cultural anthropologist Gayle Rubin, author of *Thinking Sex*. 'Whatever you enjoy sexually, somebody, somewhere will find it the most exciting thing imaginable. Perhaps we should allow ourselves to have exactly the kind of sex we want as long as everybody involved is enjoying what they are doing.'

According to a recent study by the College of Sex and Relationship Therapy (COSRT), 35% of men and 54% of women say they have problems with sex. Lack of sexual desire is the most common issue for women, and performance for men e.g. premature ejaculation and erection difficulties. Loss of libido is a perennial topic in the media. According to *Psychologies* magazine, Relate has reported a 240% increase between 1996 and 2002 in couples coming for counselling to address loss of desire. The Kinsey Institute is also about to publish a survey that suggests 21st century women are having less sex than their grandmothers.

Part of the problem is that sex is everywhere and used to sell commodities. It's in the charts (Rihanna's song *S&M*), on billboards, in movies, magazine articles, and free porn can be found on the Internet. It's how teens are learning about sex and it's easy to see how bad habits form, given that most porn is fantasy sex and far from educational. Models are airbrushed and actors chosen for their neat and tidy genitals to give us a better view. Most porn is unrealistic but it sets a precedent and can make us feel less when our bodies and sex lives don't look as exciting. The Internet has only been here for around 2,080 weekends, but it's transformed our sex lives. In less than an hour you

'Whatever you enjoy sexually, somebody, somewhere will find it the most exciting thing imaginable.'

can find casual sex, share your fantasies with a stranger, and investigate your local swinging and fetish scene. It can generate more anxiety because there's a cultural pressure to be adventurous, to find the next exciting thing and value quantity over quality.

If you want to improve your sex life it's helpful to think about it in the context of your relationship rather than something separate that you 'do'. Good sex is related to communication and intimacy so if you're experiencing a dip in libido it's a sign that there are things you need to talk about. Often we avoid talking about sex because we don't want to upset our lovers. So, actions become habits, which are then hard to break. If you're bored with the routine take the initiative and think about what *you* really, really want. It sounds basic but women tend to put everyone else first and we aren't always the best at asking for what we need.

'Don't panic if you're not having much sex. Try to see it as cyclical, an ebb and flow that will return.'

Feeling bored with life (and sex as part of that) is normal and it happens to all of us at some point, particularly in long-term relationships, says Susan Quilliam, sex therapist and author of *The New Joy of Sex*. Don't panic if you're not having much sex. Try to see it as cyclical, an ebb and flow that will return. She believes that drought reignites desire so if you've reached an impasse, let any expectations and pressure go. Stop initiating sex for a short period of time and focus on other types of conscious touch. Or ban touching altogether for a period of time to build anticipation and reignite your desire.

Pamela Lister, author of *Married Lust* believes there are 10 secrets to good sex – enthusiasm, variety, adventure, generosity, authenticity, attention, courage, confidence, attraction and delight. 'Contrary to myth, desire is not born in the genitals but in the mind and in the soul, and therefore it has the potential for unlimited growth and renewal with the same person. But for the thrill to rise, for the idea of yearning and lust to constantly renew itself, you've got to set the conditions. Get rest. Get a life. And clear out the cobwebs in your mind so that there's actually some room for desire to grow. The secret to long-lasting lust is not about multi-orgasmic sex in hot tubs, it's not to try to be sexier. Desire is fed by intimacy, which is fed by expressing the truth about ourselves in and out of the bedroom.'

'Good sex doesn't just happen. You've got to make it happen, like anything else in life,' says Esther Perel, author of *Mating in Captivity*. 'Put as much effort into your erotic life as you do your work and social life and see what happens.'

Planning kinky things will give you energy, a sense of purpose and something to look forward to, and this will feed into your desire. Like a bank account, your sex life needs regular deposits to grow. Set up an account called 'Pleasure' and make regular deposits to spend on things that give you joy and feed your erotic mind. Invest in your relationship and you will both reap the benefits, as intimacy will deepen.

Keep a pillow book and note down any desires, fantasies and triggers that turn you on. This will help you stay mindful and present, as so often we're spectators during sex, our minds jumping ahead to the next thing. Make time to sit down together and talk properly every day. *The Times'* sex columnist, Suzi Godson, recently said, 'Couples that talk about sex won't be bored with sex.'

A friend of mine has been delighting me with tales of her new lover and the great sex they are having so I asked her what does it for her. 'Eye contact whatever position we're in. I've never communicated with a man so much during sex. It's so refreshing.' Small changes make a difference she says, like having sex at the other end of the bed. 'It was like being in a different room and we saw each other's bodies from a different angle.'

'Good sex involves a physical, psychological, emotional and spiritual connection.'

Good sex involves a physical, psychological, emotional and spiritual connection. We're never too old to learn a new trick or two, so if you're curious to learn a bit more about different sex styles and pleasure/pain rituals I've included a few ideas to help you explore. Here's to more juicy pleasure in your life. Have fun exploring each other!

I'd love to hear your feedback, comments and suggestions for my research. You can reach me via email: nicci@inrudehealth.com.

Disclaimer

This book contains adult material intended for over 18s only. It has been written for educational and entertainment purposes and does not aim to diagnose medical problems. If you are concerned about any aspect of your health, please see your GP.

Chapter One

Sex and Intimacy

'Good sex? Ooh, that's a *huge* topic,' said my friend when I told her the title of this book. 'How are you going to narrow it down?' It's a good question because sex means different things to different people, and what we define as 'good sex' is a matter of personal preference based on our experiences to date. My aim is to give you information on several aspects of sexual pleasure, including intimacy, kink, orgasms, sex positions, aphrodisiacs and foreplay, so you can dip in and take bits that are relevant and helpful to you. If a certain topic piques your interest then check the help list at the back of the book and you'll find further resources. Sex is a broad canvas so I've tried to focus on specific areas.

Earlier this year I put together an online survey asking couples what a healthy sex life means to them. The comments are fascinating and I've printed the quotes in chapter 11. Most of you said that it's important to prioritise sex, to not try and squeeze it in at the end of the day when you're both too tired to enjoy it. That means going with the flow, be it a lunchtime quickie or a weekend tantric workshop where you can really indulge one another. Common phrases that define good sex: fun, trust, freedom, communication, passion and adventure.

Widen the scope of what 'sex' is and let go of the idea that it's a three-course meal to orgasm. You don't feel like eating the same foods in the same setting and style every day so why should sex be any different?

Improving your sex life

Sex coach, Dr Tara Few says her work has consistently shown her that the best improvement in the quality of a couple's sex life comes from taking emotional risks and being confident enough to communicate what you like. In other words, focusing on technique, performance and frequency won't bring you

'Open communication is an essential part of good sex. Sex needs to be varied; sometimes it might be gentle and sensual, and sometimes it might be vigorous and active. It's always 'doing' sex in the same way that leads to deadness and difficulty in maintaining good sex in a long-term relationship.'

good sex if you aren't getting what you need and if you're not being true to your sexual self. Working out what you need is a lifetime's play and different sexual partners show us new sides of ourselves that we may wish to explore.

Expanding your repertoire via positions, props, technique and frequency is the focus of most magazine articles on 'hot sex' because we like to think of ourselves as adventurous, and 'sexy' sex sells! Being intimate, open, vulnerable and learning how to communicate what we need to be happy are what make sex really hot. If you can both give unconditionally, without expectation or judgement then you can reach the spiritual heights of sex, which are life-enhancing and transformational. It's a lifetime's journey and one that is challenging and fun. You may need to step outside your comfort zone from time to time, but new experiences help us to grow as people.

Common issues around sex

Dr Few explains that the following issues are common ones that arise in her coaching work:

- Sexual frequency – i.e. one of you wants more sex than the other. She suggests trying to work out an ideal frequency and finding a level that you are both happy with. If your sex drive has dipped recently can you pinpoint when and why it happened?

- Sexual positions – despite the plethora of exciting positions out there most of us tend to have 1-3 in our repertoire because they're comfortable, easy and get us from A-B in the shortest time. That's fine but not every time. If you're in a bit of a rut, ban sex from the bedroom and take it into a different arena – use sex furniture, go outdoors, drive off somewhere in the car. Studies show that one new encounter or small change makes all the difference to how adventurous you both perceive your sex life to be.

- Communication – good sex is about being able to say what you really want, how you want it and how often. Express it in a way that isn't negative to your lover but enhances what he or she is already doing – a new suggestion instead of a criticism. Be true to yourself and own your fantasies and desires even if they don't match your lover's at this moment. Communication is something that we get better at over time with age, experience, confidence and lovers. It's also about knowing your own body so you're aware that how you like to be touched can vary depending on where you are in your hormonal cycle. Tell your lover these things and he'll know in advance not to play with your nipples when you have your period. We are cyclic creatures and knowing your body and moods throughout the month is helpful when it comes to expressing what you want.

- Communication is also about knowing your yes/no boundaries and when to say no if something isn't doing it for you or you're not in the mood for a certain activity. A facilitator at a goddess workshop I attended said, 'I forgive myself for all those times I had sex when my pussy was dry.' Her comment raised a few knowing chuckles and it reiterates the point that sometimes it's easier to go with the flow to keep a lover happy when we really feel like saying no.

- Be open, vulnerable and committed to a journey of emotional discovery to find out about each other, otherwise you can reach stalemate. Talk about your sex life regularly (outside of the bedroom preferably) with diplomacy, tact, and non-judgement and without defensiveness. Listen well. It's easy to get into the habit of thinking you know exactly how to bring each other to orgasm. Be mindful that sexual responsiveness changes every day. Tantra teacher, Rebecca Lowrie, said recently at a workshop on conscious touch, 'When my partner and I first got together he wasn't sure if he wanted to be monogamous, he thought he might like to be with other women. We began to explore concious sexuality, really being present with each other in every moment. After a while he said that he didn't need to be with other women because being fully present with me meant I was new in each moment.'

- Approach sex from a place of abundance and spirit of generosity, as what you give out you get back. This is the basic law of attraction theory explored by authors Jerry and Esther Hicks and Rhona Byrne. Be mindful that your thoughts create your reality so focus on what you want rather than what you don't want!

What do you really want?

Here's a quick exercise from Joanne Morrow PhD, a sex educator at Vulva University, to help you identify who you are leaning on the most, who gives you support and how balanced your relationships are. Make a list with two columns to help you identify what your physical and emotional needs are at this moment. In the left hand column write down your needs and in the right hand column write down who fulfils them. Sex therapists say that when we lean too heavily on our lovers for emotional support it can have an effect on the level of desire they feel for us. Simply put, one person can't take on all of our needs and still desire us. Families are fragmented and we no longer have the same support networks and communities around us so we tend to depend on a smaller band of people. Be selective and mindful about whom you offload to and how often. If it's a big issue consider talking to a counsellor for an impartial opinion. This will make you feel lighter and you'll have more energy to bring to your relationship. It creates more space between you for desire to thrive.

It's an empowering exercise to assess how well you are handling your issues, needs, and how well the power is balanced in your intimate relationships.

Passion coach Vena Ramphal runs a course with Sacred Pleasures on identifying what you really want from your relationship. It includes a yin/yang ritual and exercises in asking for what you want. For further details see the help list.

Efficient Vs amazing sex

Dr Few points out that back in the 1970s, sex researchers Masters & Johnson did a piece of research called *Persons Studied in Pairs*. They assessed straight, gay, short and long-term couples to find out what made sex amazing and concluded that sex can be both efficient (goal-setting and orgasm) and amazing. The gay couples reported the most amazing sex and the couples in long-term relationships were also more satisfied. They concluded that brief encounters can be steamy and indulge our fantasies, but in the long run knowing someone's body intimately and having the time to explore each other and find out what turns you on is key to a satisfying sex life.

Their good sex tip then is to slow things down and take your time with arousal and foreplay. Learning how to tease is an art form. Burlesque lessons will teach you how to speak with your eyes and 'conceal and reveal'. Suspense is the basics of theatre, drama and art – learning how to build tension to pull the audience in. Why not initiate sex when you're both fully dressed? Learn how to wake up your whole body so that when you do orgasm it will be a full body one. Tantric and Taoist techniques and kink play can show you new ways to do this.

Being more adventurous

A sex worker friend says it's worth trying something new three times – first to figure out how to do it, second to see if you like it and third so it feels natural. He made me laugh but it's a valid point. We tend to give up if a sex position or technique is challenging and doesn't do it for us right away, but, like any new skill, it takes time to pick things up. If you've tried anal sex and didn't like it try it again a different way and see how you feel about it. Sex therapist and author Gabrielle Morrissey suggests trying a new position three times a week before moving on to something else or bringing in props. This is because familiarity makes something feel more natural and when something feels natural you are more likely to enjoy it.

Make a sex wishlist at the start of the week and order a new toy or prop. Internet shopping is speedy so it creates a sense of anticipation for what's to come. It's also a nice way to burn off the Monday blues! Make a list of fantasies you'd like to explore and exchange lists. Betty Herbert has written a book called *The 52 Seductions*, which is full of innovative and fun ideas.

Developing intimacy

We all crave intimacy but it can also be a bit scary because it challenges deeper parts of our personality and means being open, vulnerable and letting our masks slip. Ava Cadell, sex therapist and founder of Loveology University, points out the word 'intimacy' can be broken down into 'In Two Me see' so it's about shared moments, trust, safety, closeness, transparency, empathy and vulnerability. 'Intimacy is not just sex but incorporates trust, comfort, safety, surrender and respect to open communication. The sexiest thing for a woman is when her man is fully focused and present with her when he is making love to her. Both partners must have a clear intention of fullness in the moment rather than being goal-oriented.'

Joanne Morrow PhD, a sex educator at Vulva University, explains that intimacy is the 'mutual sharing of thoughts and ideas, emotions, touch, and psychic and energetic connections'. 'The joy of it,' she says, 'is that as we age we realise there are many levels of intimacy so think of it as unwrapping each other daily and getting to know each other on different levels. Intimacy is learned behaviour and it takes time and self-acceptance to be open,

'We tend to give up if a sex position or technique is challenging and doesn't do it for us right away, but, like any new skill, it takes time to pick things up.'

vulnerable and honest with one another. The key to developing it lies in self-acceptance and liking ourselves. If we are backing away from something and afraid of intimacy it can be a sign that we have low self-esteem and don't value ourselves.'

To experience deep intimacy with another you need to love and accept yourself first of all. 'Fall in love with yourself and be your own best friend,' says Joanne, and know yourself on all levels – physical, spiritual, emotional and mental. Work through any self-esteem issues that are holding you back from sharing yourself fully.

Things to try

Here are a few pointers from Joanne on how to deepen intimacy. I recommend the online courses at Vulva University, as they are full of inspiring ideas:

- Fantasy sex is the basis for kink play. Find a mutual fantasy or story and re-enact it, with costumes or without, at home or elsewhere. Being vulnerable, free and open about your desires deepens intimacy. Jay Wiseman, author of *Tricks to Please a Man* suggests taking it in turns to create a dialogue/story, which describes your play as a way to stimulate creativity and desire.

- Aural trysts – if the thought of phone sex makes you squirm with embarrassment then there are some great books out there to help you overcome your inhibitions. I recommend Barbara Keesling's *Talk Sexy to the One You Love* and Carol Queen's *Exhibitionism for the Shy*. Barbara suggests getting down to it during masturbation by letting out a stream of consciousness. You may feel a bit self-conscious at first but you'll soon get into it and it feels quite liberating. Experts think opening the throat makes orgasms more powerful.

- Exchange life stories about sex – find out what your lover's upbringing was around sex, any hang-ups, and whether he or she grew up in a sex-positive house. This will deepen your understanding of his or her sexual response and ensure that any negative experiences aren't repeated.

- Say thanks every day for small things and be in a state of love and gratitude. Saying thanks for the domesticities creates emotional space between you because you are physically acknowledging your separateness. It creates an energy flow that feels good and strengthens your bond. Over time this will build a sense of love, generosity and appreciation, which will feed into your sex life. Emily Dubberley, author and sexpert at www.tickled.co.uk suggests 'praising your partner because you *want* to praise him or her, not because you're hoping to get a compliment in return. It may sound obvious but all too many people say "I love you" when what they really mean is "Tell me that you love me". Give compliments freely without expectation and you'll build the intimacy in your relationship. It takes seven compliments to balance one criticism so it could well help ease the tension in your relationship too'.

Summing Up

■ Widen the scope of what 'sex' is and let go of the idea that it's a three-course meal to orgasm. Be prepared to take emotional risks and get out of your comfort zone to communicate what you really want and need. Being intimate, open and vulnerable, and having an intention are what make sex really hot.

■ Pay compliments and express gratitude; give unconditionally without expectation or judgement.

■ Common issues around sex include frequency, positions, and communication. Approach sex with a mindset of abundance and a spirit of generosity.

■ Intimacy is the mutual sharing of thoughts, ideas, emotions, touch, psychic and energetic connections. It's learned behaviour and it takes time to be open, honest and vulnerable with each other. The key lies in self-acceptance.

Chapter Two

The Female Body

We live in a celebrity culture and the pressure to look good and improve ourselves physically has never been greater. There's a massive focus on our external body image, says Suzi Godson, with tattoos, piercings, beauty and genital cosmetic surgery treatments on the rise. What we often don't appreciate are the inner workings of the body. She points out that an understanding of how basic biology works will improve our understanding of sex and relationships, as well as maximising sexual pleasure.

Female sexual response cycle

Masters & Johnson defined four stages of sexual response from the desire to have sex to post-orgasm:

- Excitement (or desire) – when the brain responds to a kinky thought or touch, triggering an increase of blood in the body, intensified breathing and heart rate, and a sex flush. It can take a woman up to 45 minutes to get really turned on hence the need for lots of foreplay. Her nipples get erect and the labia majora (outer lips – see diagram overleaf) flatten out, increasing in size. The labia minora (inner lips – see diagram overleaf) also get bigger and she'll have a mini clitoral erection. Her vagina swells and self-lubricates in preparation for sex.

- Plateau – the period just before orgasm when excitement is peaking. It's a shorter phase in women than men.

- Orgasm – a muscular release of tension triggering contractions in the pelvic area at around 0.8 seconds apart. A woman's orgasm lasts around 15 seconds. The vagina expands and the clitoris retracts under its hood. She may be able to go on and have multiples after her first if he stops clitoral stimulation for a while and resumes later.

■ Resolution – her muscles relax and blood pressure and breathing go back to normal. The hormone prolactin is released, leaving her feeling happy and relaxed.

Her hot spots

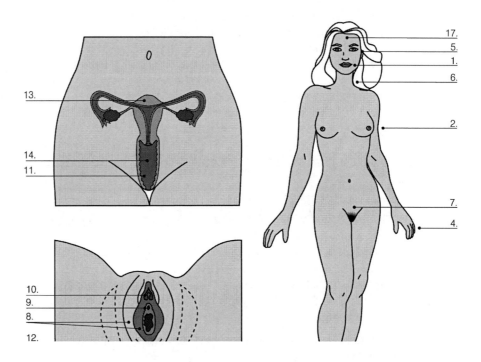

Erogenous zones are areas of the body that are rich in nerve endings, therefore sensitive to touch. The skin is our largest one and a woman's is 10 times more sensitive than a man's so she will enjoy being touched in different ways. Fleshier areas such as the buttocks and thighs respond to more intense types of touch – spanking, flogging, caning or biting – once she's warmed up! Skin sensitivity also varies depending on where she is in her hormonal cycle. Some women can't bear nipple play when they have their period. Experiment with different props – ostrich feathers, wax, ice, firesticks, champagne, silk, leather floggers, canes, oils, latex, and faux fur. The general rule of thumb with pain/pleasure is to start soft and slow and increase the pressure once the skin is warmed up and endorphins are flowing. Funnily enough, our bodies can also take more intense stimulation after a good laughing session so a bit of comedy beforehand is a good idea.

1. **Mouth, tongue and lips** – there is a link between the genitals and lower lip so when he kisses and gently nibble her lips she will feel it in her clitoris, enhancing arousal. Ten minutes of intense snogging will prepare her body for sex.

2. **Breasts and nipples** – nipple clamps provide a more intense sensation and will heighten orgasm as they give you a little head rush when you take them off. Warm up the area first with breast massage and don't forget to include the whole breast tissue extending to the armpit, as this is also very sensitive.

3. **Feet and toes** – in reflexology the ankle area relates to reproduction and sexuality, so you can ease any blockages by massaging here. Feet are also sensual and powerful and tap into (no pun intended) any foot fetishes. Seeing a woman in kinky leather boots is a turn on for many men. Our feet are covered in nerve endings to help us balance and find our footing. Passion coach, Vena Ramphal, suggests giving yourself a loving foot massage regularly to help you appreciate all of your body. A footbath at the end of the day is a nice bit of foreplay, so pay attention to the delicate skin between the toes, as this feels sensual when stroked.

4. **Hands and fingers** – the skin between the fingers and hands is highly sensitive to touch so lock your fingers together when you hold hands. Our wrists and palms are also responsive. Sexpert, Tracey Cox, suggests a sexy way to give a woman 'oral sex' in public – lick, gently nibble and suck the palm of her hand, and she can do the same for her man by licking and sucking his fingers.

'Experiment with different props – ostrich feathers, wax, ice, firesticks, champagne, silk, leather floggers, canes, oils, latex, and faux fur.'

5. **Scalp and ears** – The scalp is covered in nerve endings, so an Indian head massage will increase blood flow to the brain, release dopamine and serotonin, and relax her. I love it when a man holds my head and pulls my hair – it feels very erotic, especially if he slowly drips warm oil onto my forehead.

6. **The neck, throat and collarbone** – most women love the back of their neck being kissed, rubbed and tickled and when touched like this she feels it all the way down her spine.

7. **The pubic area** includes the clitoral hood, vulva and vaginal entrance, urethral opening, perineum and anus – the main hot spots for a woman once he's completed steps 1-6. The vulva (mons veneris) is the term for the entire external area of the vagina and generally responds to firm touch. Try cupping the entire area with your hand before you leave the house – it's a sexy way to take 'ownership' and remind her of what's to come later. I've found my vulva is a lot more sensitive to oral sex and massage after shaving my pubic hair and men seem to prefer it hair-free. It's personal preference. Pubic hair does have a role to play in that the scent trapped by the hair emits pheromones, the chemicals our bodies produce to attract a mate.

8. **Labia** – the labia majora and minora are both sensitive and contain sweat glands so aid the release of pheromones. The labia minora are there to protect the clitoris, urethra and vagina and provide additional stimulation for the penis when he moves in and out of her vagina. They are an extension of the vagina if you like, so it's not a great idea to tamper with them for the sake of aesthetics (I'm referring to labial reduction surgery as we don't know what the long-term effects of this are in terms of pleasure and sexual response). I think of the inner and outer labia as homologous to the mouth and I can't imagine having a nip 'n' tuck there so I don't really understand the trend for vaginal 'rejuvenation' unless it's for medical purposes. Check out sculptor Jamie McCartney's *Great Wall of Vagina* for an idea of how different our labias really are. It's a cast of 400 vulvas (mine is in there somewhere) from willing volunteers. We are all *so* different down there and it's refreshing to see. I'm hoping he'll do one for penises next.

9. **Urethral opening** – the tiny opening that sits between the vagina and clitoris to expel urine. Some women find it pleasurable to touch, though I can't say I've ever been too aware of it unless I've had a bout of cystitis.

10. **Clitoris** – the external part of the clitoris is pea-shaped and can be exposed by gently pulling the skin back at the top of the labia. It's protected by a hood of skin and contains 8,000 nerve endings (twice the amount of the penis) so is there purely to give us pleasure. Australian urologist, Helen O'Connell, recently discovered that it extends back much further into the body than we thought (think of a wishbone with legs) so it seems that all orgasms are clitoral in origin. What's interesting is that the size and placement of it will differ, so each lover is a voyage of discovery. I recently had my clitoris 'cupped' with surgical glass cups during a BDSM workshop. They made a seal on my skin, trapping air, and increased the size of my clitoris. It sounds bizarre but felt very pleasurable. It's a form of chastity play, as I was pinned in place and massaged by the person holding the cup before release.

11. **Vagina** – shaped like a barrel, muscular and like the diaphragm it closes flat when not in use. It expands during sexual arousal and childbirth. The first couple of inches of the vagina are the most sensitive part so shallow penetration or finger play feels good. Mix this up with deeper thrusts to stimulate the cervix at the top of the vagina – another sensitive area for women. This can feel pleasurable when she's having her period, as the lining of the womb is thicker and extra-sensitive (orgasms are also great at getting rid of period pains!). The inner folds of the vagina are called reggae, so music to your ears! Like any muscle it needs regular touch, massage and exercise to keep it healthy and ensure the tiny glands inside lubricate during arousal.

'The inner folds of the vagina are called reggae, so music to your ears!'

12. **PC muscle** – this is a hammock of muscles that holds all of the internal reproductive organs in place. It's vital to keep it strong and healthy as age, childbirth, weight and gravity all weaken it. Wearing pads for light adult incontinence is pretty common amongst younger women and part of the problem is that women aren't given much direction post-childbirth. I use a jade love egg as part of my sexual energy practice and recently did an excellent workshop with Uta Demontis at Coco de Mer to learn how to use it. It's a sensual, healing way to do your pelvic exercises and will improve sex for both of you. Stronger PC muscles allow a woman to milk a man's penis when he's inside her so a set of love eggs from Coco de Mer would make a very thoughtful gift.

13. **Womb (uterus)** – The Society for Human Sexuality describes this as a closed fist, which is helpful in visualising its size. It has three layers – myometrium, endometrium and perimetrium. When a woman has her period, the outer layer thickens so sex can feel more sensitive, particularly if he thrusts deep on certain strokes.

14. **The G-spot** – unlike the prostate gland this isn't a specific area but a sensitive pleasure zone 1-2 inches inside the vagina along her upper wall. Jaiya and Jon Hanauer (The New School of Erotic Touch) point out that every woman's G-spot is different because we have varying levels of sensitivity based on biomechanics, biochemistry, emotional development and scar tissue.

    'The G-spot has a head, body and tail that make up the entire area. The head is the urethral opening. You can see this just above the vaginal opening. It is a tiny hole from which urine or ejaculate is expelled. The body of the G-spot goes by different anatomical names – the female prostate or urethral sponge. It is located on the front wall of the vagina if a woman is lying down. This is a tube of erectile tissue that surrounds the urethra and fills with fluid during arousal. The important thing to note is that women have higher concentrations of this sensitive tissue in three different areas. For the majority of women, most of the erectile tissue is near the opening of the vagina, the second place is further inside near the G-spot tail, and the third area is in the centre of the urethral sponge.

    'The G-spot tail is about 3-4 inches inside the vaginal cavity on the front wall (also known as the A-spot or anterior fornix zone).' This area can also be responsive. They point out that G-spot stimulation can produce varying sensations so it might not feel as sexy as we expect it to. Needing to pee is classic so it's best if she empties her bladder and puts a protective sheet down before any G-spot play. It may also feel numb or painful depending on whether she has any trauma, scar tissue or recent infection in the area; whether she's turned on; where she is in her menstrual cycle, and how emotional she is. I suffered from vaginismus in my 20s, which made finding my G-spot a challenge because I was too tight and afraid of the pain to really let go, enjoy self-stimulation and ejaculate. Giving myself time and permission to do so has been a revelation and helped me to open my body to pleasure. I recommend trying G-spot massage with a finger and toy to appreciate the differences in sensation. Insert a finger palm side up when you're aroused and press it into the tissues on the top of the vaginal wall. Try to visualize moving and stimulating the tissue to give yourself an internal massage. Try different strokes and vary the pressure. After enough stimulation the area will feel quite hot and feel like it's opening up. It can lead to intense full body orgasm that feels different to clitoral orgasms; possibly because it's stimulating two nerve pathways. Read Deborah Sundahl's book *G-spot and The Art of Female Ejaculation* for more tips and a history of the G-spot.

15. **Perineum** – this is the area of stretchy skin between the vagina and anus. Midwives recommend massaging it prior to childbirth to help prevent tearing and it also feels pretty pleasurable to touch so experiment with lubricant.

16. **Anus** – a hot spot full of nerve endings, which responds to external and internal touch. Try rimming using a dental dam and gentle finger massage on the exterior before internal massage. The key to good anal sex is taking your time and using lots of lubricant, as the anus doesn't lubricate. Wearing latex gloves is recommended to avoid scratches or tearing of the delicate tissues inside the anus (also good for tapping into any medical fetish fantasies). Try inserting your index finger and once it's inside stop what you are doing and wait until the sphincter relaxes. The anus has two sphincters – one she can relax and the other automatically tightens so it can take time for the body to relax and get used to the sensation. Once she's happy with the sensation of a finger she can move on and try butt plugs during sex, other anal toys or anal penetration using a condom and lots of lube. Some women love anal play and others hate it. I'd say go by the three-times rule – try any sexual activity three times in different ways to see if you like it before dismissing it. It may be that the technique wasn't right first time around. There are lots of good books on anal play. I recommend Tristan Taormino and Jack Morin. Sh! Womenstore also run workshops on anal and P-spot play.

17. **The Brain** – Daniel Amen, a neuroscientist based in the US (www. amenclinics.com) describes it as a 'chemical factory looking for love'. It's our primary pleasure centre as it controls sexual response through the release of love chemicals, hormones and neurotransmitters during attraction and love. Research has shown that during orgasm the areas of our brain responsible for fear and anxiety shut down enabling us to really let go and enjoy the pleasure of sex. This is nature's way of ensuring survival of the species I imagine. When

we meet someone we like, the release of chemicals (epinephrine and norepinephrine) can make sex feel wildly exciting and you're in lust. This phase lasts for up to 18 months and then chemical production slows down and is replaced by feelings of safety and comfort. Sexpert, Tracey Cox, points out that it's impossible for this cocktail of chemicals to co-exist or else we'd get nothing done! Infatuation chemicals reduce as attachment chemicals increase. This is a positive thing in terms of relationships and commitment, but it can make sex feel less exciting as our brains respond to danger and adrenaline, associating this with hot sex.

Recreating desire

'Simply having sex somewhere different and new will stimulate your brain to rediscover the lusty chemicals.'

You can trick your brain to re-engage by taking risks – try new activities and adventures, business ventures, co-projects, watching a scary film, and exploring kinky play. Simply having sex somewhere different and new will stimulate your brain to rediscover the lusty chemicals. Spending time apart is also essential to enable room for desire to grow. Keep yourself tuned in sexually by writing an erotic diary, exploring erotica online and finding out what turns you on – an ongoing, changing process. Develop your powers of fantasy so that you can have an orgasm through fantasy alone – no touch allowed. This is very empowering (and useful for long journeys).

Secondary erogenous zones

You can create a secondary erogenous zone by stroking a particular area of her body after she's had an orgasm. This will create an association of pleasure in her mind so that in future, she will be turned on when you touch her there.

Summing Up

- A woman has four stages of sexual response – excitement, plateau, orgasm and resolution, and generally needs around 45 minutes of foreplay to be really ready for sex.

- The whole body is an erogenous zone and female skin is 10 times more sensitive than men's. Experiment with different types of touch and props. Wake up her whole body first and she's more likely to experience a full body orgasm from clitoral, vaginal or anal touch.

- The brain is our biggest sex organ, responsible for the release of hormones and chemicals that make us feel lust, infatuation and committed love. It's possible to recreate the early heady days by exploring new activities together.

Chapter Three

The Male Body

Sex therapist, Dr Ian Kerner, says the entire male body is an erogenous landscape not just the obvious bits. I've found this with nipple play – an ex was surprised to find it turned him on when I gently bit and sucked his nipples so it became a regular part of our play. Male skin is less sensitive than a woman's so can handle a firmer touch and massage. The hairier a man is, the less sensitive his skin will be generally and the more massage oil he'll soak up so it's only polite that he shave his back, sack and crack in return.

You can learn a lot about how a man likes to be touched and his sexual response system by watching him masturbate. Unlike yours, his bits are easily accessible and he's well acquainted with handjobs. Most men love oral sex and it's something they can't do for themselves (unless they are exceptionally yogic). If he's trained himself to come too quickly in fear of being caught then this can contribute to premature ejaculation. To counteract this he needs to slow things down to retrain his body so he can hold more sexual tension before releasing it. He can also teach himself how to separate orgasm and ejaculation through masturbation – it's called 'edgeplay' and it's something a woman can help with.

'Male skin is less sensitive than a woman's so can handle a firmer touch and massage.'

Male sexual response cycle

His sexual response cycle is similar to hers except things happen a little bit quicker:

▪ Excitement – stimulation from a kinky thought or touch triggers his brain to release blood in the body. Heart and blood rate increases, as does blood pressure. His nipples become erect and he develops a sex flush on his chest. His brain sends a message to his penis stimulating an erection, his scrotum thickens and the testicles draw upwards.

- Plateau – this is the period just before orgasm. Heart and blood circulation increases to 180 beats per minute, so he'll sweat more and feel ultra-sensitive to touch. The main difference between this phase in women and men is that he gets excited more quickly and he has a longer plateau before orgasm. Muscles at the base of the penis contract and his glans swells.

- Orgasm – In men the processes of orgasm and ejaculation are separate events, so he can come without ejaculating. His penis contracts and he is at the point of no return when he can't hold back any longer. His pelvic muscles contract, moving fluid through the urethra and semen spurts out of the tip of the penis.

- Resolution – After orgasm his muscles relax and blood pressure returns to normal. Prolactin is released leaving him relaxed and contented. He then goes into a refractory period (rolling over and falling asleep) and he can't have sex or get an erection again for a period of time – minutes, hours or days depending on his age!

'Orgasm is a physical response to the build-up of muscular tension.'

Post-40 a man's erections are less firm and he needs direct stimulation to get an erection. The refractory period can be frustrating for a woman because she can continue to peak after her first orgasm. So it's only polite that he lets her come first. It's not always a bad thing because it makes older men more creative and thoughtful lovers. They are happy to focus on female pleasure and have mastered the art of separating orgasm and ejaculation so that sex can last longer.

Edgeplay

Orgasm is a physical response to the build-up of muscular tension. It's a rhythmic release that feels highly pleasurable. It can be a dry orgasm e.g. a prostate orgasm, or a wet one when a man ejaculates. Ejaculation is a reproductive response and semen is expelled a couple of seconds post orgasm. He can learn how to orgasm without ejaculating to prolong his pleasure – and hers – holding back will lead to an accumulation of sexual energy and a more intense orgasm.

Here are two techniques to prevent ejaculation from Dr Andrew Stanaway, author of *Erotic Massage for Lovers.* He explains that it can take a few weeks to perfect so be patient. He needs to start solo and then you can try it together.

Stop/start technique

▨ Masturbate for 15 minutes with a dry hand and try not to ejaculate. The aim is to sense your point of no return at which you can't hold back ejaculation. Gauge your arousal level on a scale of 1-10 so you know how close you are.

▨ When you're about to ejaculate stop all stimulation and focus on the feeling in your genitals. Take a few deep breaths and wait for a while before you resume stimulation.

▨ Repeat this cycle several times until you can last 15 minutes. Once you've mastered this add lube and try again. Lube is arousing so this will be more challenging.

The big squeeze

▨ Pleasure yourself to the point of no return then squeeze just below the rim of the glans with your finger and thumb until your erection diminishes.

▨ Repeat this cycle several times and notice how much sexual energy is building in your pelvic area.

▨ Repeat using lubricant until you are able to last as long as you want to.

Other techniques he suggests include altering the way you thrust – deeper thrusting will be less stimulating as the glans of the penis is further inside her vagina where it's less tight. Think about other things and visualise yourself lasting as long as you want.

Sexual homology

Although our genetic sex is established at conception (by the male sperm), during the first few weeks of fetal development our internal and external genitalia are the same. The default sex is female and when our organs develop is determined by the presence of testosterone. The SRY gene initiates male sexual differentiation and testosterone stimulates the development of the genitals – gonads become testicles or ovaries, phallus becomes a clitoris or penis, and genital folds become labia or scrotum. This process has normally happened by the 12th week of pregnancy, so we can identify sex of a baby at a 16 or 18 week scan. It's helpful to remember that men come from women and that our intimate bits are homologous tissues.

The Society For Human Sexuality explains that these homologous parts will feel similar in terms of sensation when touched. The glans of the penis is related to the glans of clitoris. It's nice to find the bits that are equally as sensitive because how she likes to be touched is how he'll also enjoy being touched in these areas. The clitoris is a miniature version of the glans of penis – small but powerful in that it contains twice the number of nerve endings – 8,000 instead of 4,000. I think to make up for fact that women have the tough deal with periods and childbirth!

The clitoral wings (crura) are like the internal parts of the penis (the corpora cavernosa) so if you visualise it splitting into two legs like a wishbone then it resembles the penis internally. Think of the clitoral glans as an active player during sex – it gets it own erection and swells in size. His prostate gland and her G-spot are also homologous so it's helpful to learn how to give each other a G-spot and P-spot massage.

The following table matches his bits to hers in terms of sensitivity. Touching each other on the visible bits is a nice intimate exercise to do and reminds us of how similar we really are.

Male	Female
Glans of penis	Glans of clitoris
Corpora cavernosa	Clitoral body and crura (wings)
Corpous spongiosum	Vestibular bulbs
Prostate gland	Skene's glands (inside urethral sponge)
Shaft of penis	Labia minora
Scrotum	Labia majora
Testicles	Ovaries
Foreskin	Clitoral hood
Cowper's glands	Bartholin's glands

Source: Society For Human Sexuality – sexuality.org

His hotspots

The external hotspots are similar in both sexes so I've focused on his reproductive areas here:

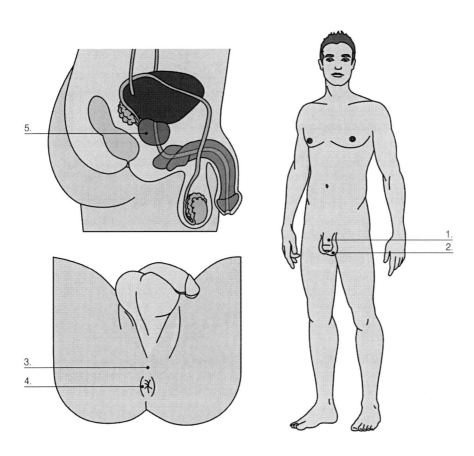

1. **The penis** – has three internal parts to give him an erection. Two corporal cavernosa and one corpus spongiosum. It's made up of spongy tissues, which engorge with blood to give him an erection. The glans is the most sensitive area and is covered with foreskin in uncircumcised males. This is followed by underside – coronal ridge and frenulum – the ridge on back of penis, which joins the shaft and glans. The penile raphe is the ridge running down the underside of shaft, which is also very sensitive. His urethral tube produces pre-cum a few seconds before he ejaculates. Foreskin is receptive and feels good when pulled back over the glans or pinned in place before oral sex.

2. **Scrotum** – houses his testicles. It's a sensitive area and most men love it when it's cupped and gently tugged during oral sex. It's there to regulate the temperature of his testicles so that sperm can survive and do their job. Spreading his legs and gently tugging his testicles can delay ejaculation. Most men appreciate firm touch here and a spot of vibrator play also feels nice.

3. **Perineum** – the spot between the base of his penis and the anus. It is full of nerve endings and home to the 'million dollar spot' according to Taoist sexual practice. Try massaging or licking it during oral sex.

4. **Anus** – also highly pleasurable for many men. Try rimming or fingering the area lightly at first and then massage internally with your finger or a prostate toy once he's aroused. This will indirectly stimulate the base of the penis or prostate gland. Use latex gloves, lots of lube and go slowly. Always use a dental dam for rimming. It's also worth buying a good P-spot toy such as the Aneros Helix so he can see how different it feels. There are many happy men talking about the Aneros on sex forums! It's anatomically designed to stimulate the prostate but takes a bit of practice to get right. Once he's familiar with it he can try leaving it in during sex or masturbation for added stimulation.

5. **Prostate gland** – This produces part of the fluid that makes up semen and closes the urine duct at orgasm so that sperm can move properly. It's located just inside the anus – a finger's width in and feels like a small dome. Many men find P-play highly pleasurable and if he's not tried it yet it's likely to be a whole new pleasure zone. Prostate massage has lots of benefits – it's good to orgasm regularly and it helps him to produce more ejaculate, keeping the prostate healthy.

How to give him a prostate massage

Go slowly – massage his body all over first to warm him up or spank his bottom to get the endorphins going. Prostate massage feels best when he's already turned on, as the prostate increases in size. Wear latex gloves to prevent any tiny tears and start slowly using lots of silicone lubricant. Ask him to lie on his front on a towel/rug or massage coach. Gently push your finger into his anus palm side up and wait for a few seconds to let his body become accustomed to the sensation. The anus has two sphincters – one we can relax voluntarily and the other tenses involuntarily so it takes a bit of time and practice.

Once inside, gently move your finger and stroke come hither, feeling for a dome-shaped area one to two inches inside. Experiment with different types of pressure and movement and ask him for feedback. One of the organisers of a prostate massage workshop with Deborah Sundahl describes the sensation of P-play as 'tiny fishes sucking on my finger. The whole area got really hot and it gave my husband an intense orgasm'. If you want to read up on the benefits of P-spot play I recommend Dr Jack Morin's book *Anal Pleasure and Health*, Ian Kerner's *He Comes First* and the DVD *Bend Over Boyfriend*, all available from www.goodvibes.com.

Summing up

- Male skin is less sensitive so can handle a firmer touch generally. Check to see how receptive he is to pleasure/pain.

- Quick masturbatory habits can be unlearned and he can learn how to slow down his orgasm and separate ejaculation and orgasm to prolong and increase pleasure for you both. Try the stop/start or the squeeze technique.

- Men and women have sexually homologous body parts so if you work out where they are it will give you a better sense of how your respective parts feel during sex.

- Prostate play is very pleasurable for most men and can give him a strong orgasm and release.

Chapter Four

Foreplay

I don't really like the term 'foreplay' – it implies prescribed steps, a starter and something you do to get you to the main 'intercourse'. 'Moreplay' would be more fitting. Foreplay can be fun as the main event – kissing, for example, I could quite happily do all day. Ditto for sensual massage. Some of my sexiest foreplay moments have been at tantra events. I once gave a yoga teacher a full body massage and when we were both completely turned on he whispered in my ear hoarsely: 'I want to have sex with you now.' The fact that we couldn't right at that moment made it all the more exciting. At another I was blindfolded and fed dessert by various men. The deprivation of sight made us less inhibited so it led to some creative feeding and touching. Both exercises were foreplay and not designed to lead to anything else.

Dr Ava Cadell describes foreplay as the first stage in our sexual response cycle because it's about activities that stimulate the mind as well as the physical body. 'It's exploration, non-coital play, anticipation, play, sexual suspense, the sensual and erotic – a connection between two people mentally, physically and emotionally that leads to a sexual connection,' she says. It could be whispering that you're not wearing any knickers and he can look but no touching, a glance across the room at a party, a gift or a kiss. The best kind of foreplay engages all of your senses and creates an energy flow between you so that you feel close even when you're not together. Just thinking of your lover raises your vibration and puts a smile on your face.

'I don't really like the term "foreplay" – it implies prescribed steps, a starter and something you do to get you to the main "intercourse". "Moreplay" would be more fitting.'

Self-seduction

Foreplay is also something you can do solo in terms of self-seduction. I'm a big fan of exercise, beauty treatments and massages for making you feel sexy and fabulous. Reflexology and Indian head massage are divine relaxers, and a spray fake tan also feels pretty sensual when you're naked. If you're well groomed you feel sexier and are more receptive to touch. Treat yourself to some gorgeous lingerie, kinky boots or a new sex toy. Self-bondage is fun and will teach you what kind of foreplay you like. Mutual masturbation is an intimate form of foreplay you can lose yourselves in together.

Finally, take a tip from sex therapist Ian Kerner. 'Studies have shown that women are more likely to be interested in sex if the house is clean, so this should be motivation enough for men to grab a mop and load the dishwasher.'

Getting started

'All too often, men and women give their lovers the foreplay that they want to give rather than the foreplay that their lover would like to receive,' says sexpert Emily Dubberley. 'A man may focus all his attention on the breasts and genitals, while a woman may spend hours leisurely caressing every inch of a man's body and neglecting the genitals. Rather than doing what you think is right, ask your lover what his or her ideal foreplay session would entail. If they're shy ask them to write it down instead – or even chat over IM, as the distance conveyed by the medium can make it easier to be honest for some people. Like it or not, men and women are different. It's only by talking that you will find out what your partner really wants.'

So here are some juicy foreplay ideas to add to your repertoire. I've not included anything on aphrodisiacs here as chapter 8 explores the connection between food and sex.

A kinky shopping trip

Plan a day of kinky shopping. London has several erotic boutiques and a Sunday fetish fair in Islington where you can browse designers and do workshops in BDSM. It's a fun way to build anticipation, especially if you've booked into a top hotel or dungeon for the night! Look for toys you can wear when you're out and about – bullet vibrators – give him the controls for a while, love eggs or body jewellery with nipple or genital clamps. Coco de Mer has a few sexy bits of body wear that will tease and tickle as you walk. Get a proper bra fitting at Rigby & Peller or Agent Provocateur.

Cultivate a (lockable!) pleasure chest for the bedroom. Items to include – lube (water-based for sex and silicone for anal play), bondage bits – a good quality flogger, DVDs, silk or cotton rope, cuffs, a blindfold, candles, clothing, stockings and toys for clitoral, vaginal and anal play. Vibrators come in all shapes and sizes so it's a matter of experimentation to see what brands you like the best. Rabbit vibrators are great for clitoral and vaginal stimulation. Bullet vibrators are designed for clitoral use and work a treat on his penis. Finger vibrators are fun for your handbag. Love eggs – wear them when you're out and about. Dildos are good for vaginal and anal play. Cock rings sometimes have a small vibrator attached for clitoral stimulation. Butt plugs and beads for anal play. Choose good quality brands that are battery and phthalate-free and made from silicone or glass. Most of the top brands are rechargeable so you don't have to faff around with batteries.

Erotic talk

I love dirty talk but I admit it's not always that easy to do, particularly when you've been together for a while. It's very powerful to hear the words 'What do you want?', to be told how desirable you are, and to hear a lover's breathing quicken after you whisper something in his ear. A friend who works as a Pro-Domme told me that she took vocal lessons to help her express herself because she was shy in bed and it bothered her that she didn't make a lot of noise. She now has a very sexy, trill whistle – various exotic bird noises coming out her throat, which sounds *very* sexy! I admire women who work on sex chat lines and are able to bring a man to orgasm using their tone of voice and imagination.

If you want to take this further I recommend *Talk Sexy to the One You Love* by Barbara Keesling, and Carol Queen's *Exhibitionism for the Shy*. Keesling suggests a simple exercise to help you let go, which is to talk dirty to yourself when you're masturbating. The idea is to let a stream of consciousness out and say whatever comes into your mind. Just keep talking and see what difference it makes to your orgasm. I tried this and found it does intensify things. Perhaps it's because opening your throat creates a better flow of energy in the body. Keesling believes that being vocal is key to experiencing a full body orgasm.

'Cultivate a (lockable!) pleasure chest for the bedroom.'

The authors explain that we often find it hard to ask for what we want and that being a 'good girl' is something that's drummed into us from an early age. Other tips include recording yourself having an orgasm and sending it to your lover, and identifying words you find sexy and using them to tell him what you are doing to yourself. I'd also suggest ringing a sex chatline to experience first-hand how sexy aural trysts can be. Betty Herbert describes how she and her husband did this in her book *The 52 Seductions*. She gave him a blow job while he rang the chatline. Probably the quickest phone call he's ever made.

Fantasy play

'Tantra is great foreplay because it's about building anticipation, awakening the senses, and deepening your connection for better sex.'

The Internet is an adult playground – female-friendly porn, erotic stories and magazines, chat rooms for fantasy play, kinky forums, and the chance to meet like-minded people locally for foursomes and moresomes. Whatever your proclivity there's a site to cater for it. Newspaper and magazine articles imply that it's sex-obsessed men looking at porn to the detriment of their relationship, but I think it's something fun you can do together as a forum for new ideas. I'm all for taking the laptop to bed for a bit of private study.

Some of the female-friendly porn producers include Anna Span, Erika Lust, Candida Royalle, and Petra Joy. Red Tube is free and has some interesting gonzo porn (amateur, home-made porn with no frills). Write down your top three fantasies and tell your lover why they turn you on. Sex writer Violet Blue suggests watching a kinky film together and maintaining a hands-off policy until it's finished. For erotic fiction I recommend Anne Rice's *Beauty* Trilogy – it's seriously hot and very well-written erotica. Passion Press features actors reading erotic stories so you can get an idea of how to use your voice seductively. Check out The Society for Human Sexuality's website www.sexuality.org for a full educational resource list.

Tantra exercises

Tantra is great foreplay because it's about building anticipation, awakening the senses, and deepening your connection for better sex. It's not just about sex but this is the element we've packaged up in the West. Most of us think of Sting and Trudi's eight-hour sex sessions and feel intimidated. Tantra's really not scary but you need to find a teaching style you feel comfortable with as some schools can be a bit airy fairy. I recommend Jewels Wingfield, Barbara Carrelas, John Hawken, Shakti Tantra and Rebecca Lowrie. You can dip your toe in as a beginner and take it as deep as you want to.

Here are some tantric exercises for foreplay:

Conscious touch

Touch is a basic human need and we need all types to feel good about ourselves. In other words, don't just touch each other sexually when you want sex. Women are more responsive to sex when they are nurtured and touched in other ways. Conscious touch is a tantric exercise you can use when masturbating or during sex. It involves sensing the energy in your hands and having an intention behind your touch to convey to your lover. It can make a simple touch or massage feel more loaded and pleasurable.

How to do it:

Lowrie recommends the following technique for conscious touch: Use one hand to touch your lover's body to begin with and rub your hands together first to feel the energy. Have an intention behind your touch, be it healing, sensual or sexual, and choose which part of your hand will express this. Fingers are sensual and palms are healing. Hold that intention in mind as you travel around your lover's body. He or she needs to close their eyes (or be blindfolded) and follow the movement trying to sense the energy/type of touch. It's a simple but powerful exercise that makes you think about how conciously you touch someone. Try it on yourself after a bath or shower or when you masturbate.

Yab Yum

This is a nice exercise to do pre-massage as it harmonises your breath and opens the body. Sit on the floor facing each other. His legs are straight out and hers are wrapped around his waist. Give each other a cuddle and focus on sensing each other's breath. The aim is to synchronise your breathing at the same time as looking into each other's eyes. It's an incredibly powerful and intimate exercise that can dissolve boundaries. You can merge and be connected at soul level via your eyes and breath. Stanaway says if you bring in touch at this point you'll experience a togetherness that is hard to beat.

Walking blindfolded

I did this exercise at a Sacred Pleasures tantra workshop and found it fun, exciting and freeing. Decide who will be the giver and receiver. The giver blindfolds the receiver and slowly leads them around the room for 15 minutes. Add music and vary the movements so it's a bit of a dance, but stay in charge and make sure they don't stumble over anything so they can really let go. It's a great exercise in trust and can really build sexual excitement because the receiver has no idea where he or she is or what's coming next. The giver can also ask the receiver to fall backwards and be caught as they fall. We don't get to let go very much in daily life so this can be a powerful and exciting way to connect.

Erotic massage

The New School of Erotic Touch has lots of videos explaining how to give various types of intimate massage – yoni, P-spot, and lingam – so is a good starting point for ideas and techniques. Start by touching yourself in sensual ways and have lots of full body massages! Tantric healer and author Kavida Rei has written a comprehensive book called *Erotic Massage*, which has lots of useful tips and techniques. She also runs practical workshops at Coco de Mer in London, which you can attend together. Group massage sessions are also fun to do at home with friends.

Here's a brief summary of a routine I learned on my ITEC holistic massage course. It's a great relaxer and you can incorporate genital massage for deeper pleasure, if you wish. I recommend investing in a decent massage couch to make the process more comfortable. Crouching on the floor is tiring and will detract from the massage. Use heated oils and towels and make sure the room is warm so you both feel comfortable naked. Ylang-ylang and sandalwood are sensual oils to add to base oil.

- Before you start, set your intention and focus on visualising and sensing the energy in your hands (rub them together first). The receiver lies face down. Start with several long, sweeping strokes (effleurage) from the base of the spine to the shoulders to relax and warm the skin. Fold your lover's arm across his back so his palm is facing upwards. This exposes the scapula beneath his shoulders; make small circles beneath the muscle to release any pressure.

- Massage his arm and hand using different techniques and then move to the other side of the couch and repeat the moves on the other side of his body.

- Move down to the base of the back, arch of hips and buttocks and increase the pressure here. The buttocks can take pummelling and heavy pressure and we hold lots of tension here.

- Work along the back of each leg using effleurage and kneading strokes. Go deep along the back of the thigh, pulling the skin taut and working the muscles to release tension. Use your thumbs along his calves and circle the ankle and foot. You can then work his feet according to preference. Include the ankles, soles and toes, and keep the pressure firm so it doesn't tickle.

- Ask him to turn over and repeat the moves on the front side finishing with a head and face massage.

A tantric painting session

Katie Sarra is an award-winning erotic artist and couples' therapist who paints sensual portraits exploring beauty, identity, relationships and sexuality. I've seen a few of her paintings and they are incredibly sensual – bodies moving together on canvas. It's a chance to explore exhibitionism and voyeurism, as Katie is a 'voyeur' in the artistic sense. She says of her work: 'I am painting the you that is bigger than self-conscious worries about body imperfections. I paint from the heart seeing you. You can be any way you are with me and rediscover feeling comfortable with your body.' Katie offers monthly sessions at Sacred Pleasures in London and is doing a charity event at Glastonbury in 2013 if you'd like to see her live work.

Mutual masturbation

This is a powerful exercise to try when you're apart if you arrange to do it at the same time. Passion coach Vena Ramphal says it's a way to create 'sex magic', which is when you both focus on something you want to manifest at the point of orgasm. By visualising that image and the sensation of how it would feel in your mind for a few minutes post-orgasm, you begin to manifest it. Masturbation is great foreplay because it keeps us connected to our sexual energy and helps us to work out what we like in terms of play. It also gives you an emotional clear

Good Sex tip:

I find Coco de Mer's Kensington boutique very inspiring in terms of décor. The walls are painted purple and there's a silver bulldog tied up with red silk bondage rope by the door. The staff have written 'Spank me' and other sexy little messages on the floorboards, walls and staircase. It brings a sense of fun and playfulness back into sex.

out and helps you to let go of things that are no longer working for you. Never underestimate the power of a good handjob beneath the table in a restaurant or when you're snuggled up in the back row of the cinema.

The art of flirting

We Brits are notoriously bad at flirting and I notice how commonplace it is when I go abroad – in Italy and Brazil particularly. Brazilian men flirt with women of all ages through talk and dance, and it's a joy to watch and receive. It brightens up your day, raises your sexual energy and is infectious because you want to give it back. It's a skill that we need to bring into our relationships to keep the energy flowing. In 1997 The Society For Human Sexuality held a flirting conference and found that there is a crossover between good listening and good flirting skills. It's impossible not to be attracted on some level to a man who pays you full attention and recalls things that you've told him after the event! We also gravitate towards people who are naturally flirtatious – open, warm and physical with us because they make us feel good.

Joyce Jillison, author of *The Fine Art of Flirting,* has the following tips: Be a good listener, be playful yet persistent, show your vulnerabilities, flirt with no expectation of reward, ask open questions and do something new each week to keep your mind stimulated (alone and together). I'd also add paying compliments to this – they really do keep you connected and feeling appreciated.

Oral pleasures

Oral sex is great foreplay and it can also be the main event and bring us to orgasm quickly. It's fast and convenient (easier to administer in public toilets than sex and doubly exciting if you tell each other you aren't allowed to make a sound). It's primal and sexy and really gives you a taste of your lover so you can pick up on pheromones, deepening the attraction. The tongue is a precise instrument, capable of delivering a wide range of sensations from wide and open lapping on the labia or shaft, to pointed and sharp flicks on the clitoris or glans. For a man oral sex feels like a warm, wet vagina.

Introduce liquids, lube, and hot/cold sensations and use your hands to heighten arousal. It's a powerful fantasy for most men. One man I dated asked me to kneel blindfolded with my hands behind my back while giving him oral sex so I had to do all of the work with my tongue. Use your mouth to hum or talk dirty to intensify the vibration on his penis. Make it mutual and give each other a surprise soixante-neuf. The key to good oral sex is finding a comfortable position as you may be there for some time.

Erotic furniture

How sensual is your home? Are there little reminders of dirty weekends away? Sensual art on the walls, colours, fabrics, rugs, cushions, scents and so on? It helps if you can take sex out of the bedroom and look for other surfaces in your home to play. Look for the kinky in domestic items – rose thorns brushed across your body feel exciting, whipped cream can be licked off your breasts, pegs make impromptu nipple or genital clamps. Ideally we'd all have a dungeon for play but it's not always possible to rig up bondage attachments to the ceiling if you live in rented accommodation. So, be creative with your furnishings. A St Andrew's Cross makes suspended bondage a possibility. A spanking bench, Chaise Longue, under bed restraints, candle light for wax play, a bathtub or shower big enough for two, an L-shaped sofa and sheepskin rugs for sprawling on; you get the idea. The aim is to stimulate your senses and mind so that when you step through the door you relax and let go of the day.

A girlfriend recently told me that she had amazing sex in a yurt – there's something about the energy flow in a round space that made the whole experience amazing. I've never had sex in a round space so it piqued my interest and has made me curious to hire one for a kinky weekend away.

'How sensual is your home? Are there little reminders of dirty weekends away? Sensual art on the walls, colours, fabrics, rugs, cushions, scents and so on?'

Summing Up

- Foreplay is the first stage in our sexual response cycle and it's about activities that stimulate the mind as well as the physical body. Think 'exploration, non-coital play, anticipation, play, sexual suspense, the sensual and erotic – a connection between two people mentally, physically and emotionally that leads to a sexual connection'. It's about activities that engage all of our senses.

- Ask your lover exactly what an ideal foreplay session would involve and vice versa. All too often we give the kind of foreplay we'd like to receive and this isn't always what our lover wants or needs at that time.

Chapter Five

Pleasure Positions

When it comes to sex positions, most of us think of the *Kama Sutra* of Vatsyayana, which was written between the 1st and 6th centuries. It's a manual about the art of living aimed at the upper crust man and despite its notoriety as a sex manual, only one chapter focused on 'congress' or pleasure positions. It gained popularity over the years and there is now a tantric focus to some of the positions. NY-based sex therapist Dr Joy Davidson points out that it describes just 22 positions yet read any popular magazine and it seems like there are more than 22,000! An Internet search brings up hundreds – some doable, others downright acrobat ('flying the trapeze' anyone!?)

Dr Davidson points out that despite the cornucopia, most of us only have two or three positions in our repertoire. We don't bother with half of them because they demand a high level of fitness and athleticism. Weight, fitness levels and flexibility will also have an impact on the type of sex we choose to have, and the subtleties of how you move together means you'll settle into your favourites. It's human nature to try things once and give up if they don't work out so Dr Davidson suggests trying one new position three times a week to give it a chance. By the third time it'll be familiar so you'll both be relaxed and more likely to enjoy it.

For inspiration, check out some of the Taoist pillow books on sex positions, Paul Jenner's *Secrets of The Kama Sutra* eBook, or *Position of the Day: Sex in Every Way* by Em & Lo. I also like Jamye Waxman's new video, shot on location at Hedonism in Jamaica. It's called *'101 Positions For Lovers'* and features real couples that look like they're enjoying themselves. Jamye says even if you stick to one position per week it will take you just under two years to get through them all so there's plenty to keep you busy.

Good Sex tip: Animals are highly creative when it comes to sex and have the ability to contort themselves into all sorts of positions. Half-an-hour of David Attenborough on TV will give you plenty of inspiration for new positions, if his dulcet tones don't send you off to sleep first.

Sex positions fall into five main styles:

- Man on top.

- Woman on top.

- Doggy style.

- Side by side.

- Standing.

The rest are simply variations on these and it's sexy to slow things down and intensify your orgasm by transitioning from one posture to the next (add a little baby oil, slip slide and off you go). It's also fun trying to keep a man inside you while you swivel from cowgirl to reverse cowgirl. In *The Adventurous Lover,* Susan Quilliam explains that whatever the position you can vary things through shifting the motion when you get there. 'In and out is just a starting point – side to side and round and round both stimulate different sections of the relevant body part and the effect varies according to who's leading the movement,' she says.

She suggests a series of Eastern tantric poses that flow into one another, or working out your own choreography. If you're planning a longer session keep plenty of lube, water, condoms etc. handy so you don't have to stop play to fetch things.

A girlfriend once told me that the best lover she's ever had was a dancer. I can second this as I had a very sexy time with a 6ft-something yoga teacher who made me weak at the knees when he lifted me up and transported me around the room. Body strength, breathing exercises, flexibility and stamina are key to inventive sex, so those yoga classes and gym workouts are useful on many levels! I'm often struck by how sexy yoga asanas are and how easily they can be adapted to please. Finally, a tip from passion coach Vena Ramphal. She says, 'I believe that in order to be a skilful lover you need to have your own repertoire of moves, positions, rhythms and patterns that suit your body. This requires practice. But what if you find that your favourite position or stroke just doesn't do it for your lover? It can be quite a thing to give up parts of lovemaking that you hold dear or of which you are quite proud. The invitation is not simply to find something new, but to be led by the workings of your lover's body. This kind of change in your repertoire is a physical practice of surrender, non-ego and fleshy newness. It's important to practise a repertoire of moves, but the deeper skill of lovemaking is in being prepared to be undone, flummoxed and made a beginner when you least expect it.'

Erotic furniture

I touched on this earlier but it's worth mentioning again as erotic furniture can really expand sex positions. Try Liberator wedges for floor work, a sex swing for bondage, a St Andrew's Cross for standing positions, or a spanking bench to lean over. Position a couple of large mirrors at either end of the room and you'll be able to watch each other whatever position you are in.

Man on top – good ol' missionary

Pros: cuddly, intimate sex.

Cons: not especially female orgasm-friendly.

Named by Christian missionaries who, after witnessing the vulgar array of sex positions practised by South Pacific natives, decided that there was only one respectable and religious way to have sex and that was 'man on top'. Much to the islanders' amusement, I'm sure. Italians call missionary sex the 'angelic' position. We love it because it's comfortable and offers full eye, lip and skin contact. However, it's not the most female orgasm-friendly position because it doesn't offer much clitoral stimulation. Using a clitoral vibrator can help.

Variations: Wrap your legs around his back and use your PC muscles to pull him in deeper or raise your legs straight like a pair of scissors to add tension and tightness to your grip. You can also drape one or both of your legs over his shoulders, which deepens penetration so he'll hit your G-spot. A pillow or wedge under your bum will alter the angle and depth of penetration. Using ankle restraints means he can pull your legs close for a snug fit or spread them further apart so that it feels like he's taking every inch of you. For added clitoral stimulation, slip on a pair of crotchless pants and position your clit vibe to go.

Woman on top

Pros: Great for clitoral and G-spot orgasm and power thighs

Cons: You need powerful thighs.

Woman on top often tops the sex surveys as position of the day. You are free to move in any way you want to take your orgasm and you can also slow things right down and tease him by changing your rhythm and style. It's a good position to help him learn his point of no return and it means that sex can last a *long* time. Psychologically, it's sexy for him to watch you take charge and you can ramp that up by tying him up and blindfolding him so he doesn't know what's coming next.

Vary your stance – arching your back and leaning towards him will put pressure on your clitoris. Leaning backwards and shifting your weight onto your hands enables you to take him in deeper for G-spot play. Sit on top of him firmly and slide him inside half erect or squat down over him – islander style – and thrust up and down or hula your hips. It's primal and he'll love the switch (as will your thighs once they get used to it!). Alter your movements to make it deep or a shallow tease. Keep him inside you and swivel around to face his feet. It's a fun position because you can do a lot with it.

It feels especially sexy when a man does several shallow thrusts followed by a long, deep one so replicate this when you're on top and see how he likes it. Flex your PC muscles around him and give him an internal squeeze to orgasm – a tantric technique called *the art of pompoir* – 'milking the lingam'. If your muscles are strong enough you'll be able to massage different parts of his penis, which feels very sexy.

Don't confine it to the bedroom either – WOT is yummy as a quickie on the sofa when you're both fully clothed. Dr Davidson points out that a mere 5 degree shift in the angle of penetration can lead to 100% enhancement of pleasure so play around with props.

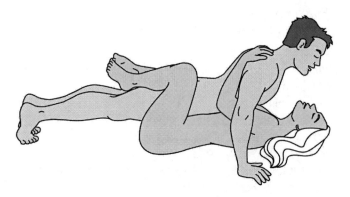

Coital alignment technique (CAT)

Good sex tip:

Slap on the baby oil in the shower for some slippery sex. It will help you to transition into some interesting positions in the bedroom.

Pros: Intense orgasm once you get the hang of it

Cons: Time, patience and practice

This is 'advanced' missionary sex devised by psychotherapist Edward Eichel in the 1990s. It requires a bit of a change in mindset, as the aim is to rock the pelvic area rather than thrusting in/out. This is more satisfying for a woman as it means her clit isn't left out.

How to do it: Penetrate her slightly with the head of your penis and keep the shaft outside of the body so that it presses against her pubic bone. Cup her shoulders with your hands and put your full body weight on her (helps if you are similar body weights). Angle your body 2-4 inches forward towards her head and concentrate on moving your weight up her body so that you brush her clitoris as you rock. Her legs should be straight out beneath yours. Rock, grind and press into each other's pelvises so that the whole pubic area is being massaged. She can pull you in more deeply by wrapping her legs around your calves. Keep it going until she comes. Eichel says CAT involves a slight adjustment in mindset, as it's not about thrusting in and out but an up and down rocking motion.

Rear entry – doggy-style

Pros: Full body orgasms, primal, great for fantasy sex.

Cons: Not much clitoral stimulation or body contact.

Casanova loved doggy-style sex. It's primal, animalistic and great for vaginal, anal and strap-on sex. You can do it standing or kneeling and it enables deep penetration, stimulating the cervix, which feels extra sexy when you have your period because the lining of the womb is thicker. It also hits the G-spot so you're more likely to have a full body orgasm. There's not much clitoral stimulation but that's easily remedied with a hand or clit vibe.

'If you want to make a small man feel bigger for both of you, opt for rear entry sex positions such as doggy style,' says Emily Dubberley, sexpert and author. 'Parting your buttock cheeks with your hands before you start will not only act as a powerful visual aphrodisiac for your man, but will also allow maximum penetration.'

There are lots of variations – bend forwards into downward dog and raise your buttocks upwards. This will lengthen the vaginal canal for deeper penetration and you'll be able to feel his testicles on your derrière. Close your legs to tighten the grip and increase friction. Put one knee on the couch and one leg on the floor . . . or make use of stairs at different heights. These moves will shorten the vaginal canal so that penetration feels fuller.

Side by side – Spooning

Pros: Cosy, good for clitoral play.

Cons: Not much depth or thrust-ability.

Spooning is ideal for those cosy sessions when you're both knackered but want to be intimate without too much physical exertion. It's also perfect for pregnancy sex, anal sex, mutual oral, and as a starting point for further activity. Try it face-to-face for kiss-ability or from behind for full body hugs. Movement is slower in this position and if your legs are slightly parted and straight he'll stay snug inside and won't be able to thrust as deeply. Spread your legs wide or hook one of them over his thighs to pull him in deeper. As with doggy-style this is good for men with a smaller penis because the position of the vagina makes entry feel fuller – the first inch or two are stimulated, which are the most sensitive areas.

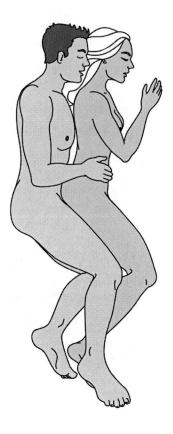

If you want to try giving him anal sex with a strap-on this is a cosy and intimate position to get you started.

Stand and deliver

Pros: Novelty factor for quickies.

Cons: Athletic and tiring.

Standing is the least common sex position according to the Kinsey Institute because it requires strength and stamina. However it's impulsive, so great for impromptu quickies when he has to have you *right now*. Try it for shower sex (non-slip mats are a must!), hotel bathrooms, or spread-eagled on the kitchen worktop with him facing you or he can push you against the wall and take you from behind. If you're shorter than him slip on a pair of heels to save his knees.

Variations – if he's in Iron Man mood get him to lift you up while you wrap your knees round his waist. Take the pressure off him a bit by leaning over the counter/sofa/bed/bonnet and arching your back. Or for a head rush try leaning backwards and putting your palms on the floor while your legs are wrapped round his waist. This can intensify orgasm if he can keep it going. Straighten your body and move your pelvis forward so that you rise to meet him – this will stimulate your G-spot.

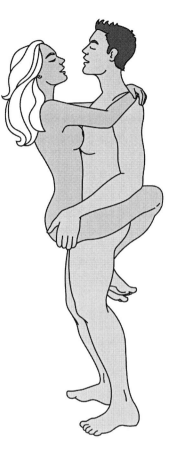

Good sex tip:

Inverted sex positions send a rush of blood to the head, which can enhance orgasm. Try hanging your head over the edge of the bed or putting your head towards the floor while he's standing with your knees wrapped around his waist.

Summing Up

- Sex positions fall into five main styles – man on top, woman on top, standing, side by side and rear entry. Despite the plethora of positions out there, most of us fall back on our favourite two or three for comfort and familiarity.

- Erotic furniture can expand your pleasure palette and take sex out of the bedroom. Explore bondage furniture and sex wedges. A slight change in motion can make 100% difference to the pleasure and sensation you both feel.

- Sex therapists recommend trying one new position three times a week to see if you really like it. Don't dismiss something if it's hard or doesn't work first time round. Fitness and flexibility determine the type of sex you can have and the more adventurous positions require higher levels of fitness. Increase the gym and yoga sessions and you'll find a whole new world of pleasure opens up.

Chapter Six

Kink Play

BDSM is an acronym for sexual power play incorporating bondage and discipline, sadomasochism, and dominance and submission. It's an alluring area of sexuality because it's a bit edgy, mysterious and risky. It involves taking yourself out of your comfort zone to explore the connection between erotic pain and pleasure, and the reward is intensified orgasms and a deeper level of intimacy than vanilla sex because you are exploring mutual fantasies and allowing vulnerabilities to surface.

It's an area of sex play that is also becoming mainstream. I read an *Independent Review* magazine article recently called *Tough Love. Unleashed: The Secret World of the Dominatrix*, which explains how popular BDSM is across many levels of society. Rihanna sings about S&M in the charts, you can now buy bondage gear (of varying quality) on the high street, and there are conferences all around the world where you can meet like-minded aficionados. The education side of kink is at the heart of BDSM play and you'll find munches (see the glossary) and workshops in most towns across the UK.

It is a big topic – books have been written about the art of Japanese rope bondage alone – so this is a general introduction to the basics of kink play.

'BDSM is an acronym for sexual power play incorporating bondage and discipline, sadomasochism, and dominance and submission.'

Types of BDSM

London Faerie runs conscious kink workshops in London and offers kinky coaching for couples. He explains that it includes the following activities:

- Impact play (floggers, hands, canes, paddles, spanking).
- Sensation play (tickling, feathers, hot wax, clothes pegs, thorns, blindfolds).
- Dominance and submission (D/S).

- Psychological role play – exploring fantasies.
- Bondage and restraints.
- Temporary play piercing or cupping.
- Experimenting with non-consent (consensually).
- Gender play.
- Age play.

Why do it?

It's adult play, fantasy time and fun! Power can be tremendously erotic. You only have to read the headlines to see that in action – high profile men on sexual assault charges. A negotiated fantasy scene where one of you is 'top' and the other 'bottom' enables you to let go, test your limits and experience the link between pleasure and erotic pain. This gives you a natural high that can be transcendental. There is a huge amount of pleasure in freedom and letting go of your day-to-day role and responsibilities for a while. It also broadens the definition of sex because BDSM and fetish isn't all about penetration – it may not come into it. It can be time enough to explore a fantasy or sensation and leave it at that level of foreplay. It's not dissimilar to tantra in that both focus on conscious touch and aim to stimulate the senses, skin, and create a deeper connection with the body. BDSM just uses different techniques and equipment.

Studies into pleasure and pain show that we like it. In 1948, Kinsey found that over ¼ of men and women in his survey had erotic responses to being bitten during sex. In 1993, Janus & Janus found 16% of men and 12% of women agreed strongly that pain and pleasure go well together in sex.

Source: Loveology University and Human Sexuality Today, 5th edition Bruce M King.

Kyree Klimist and Mikaya Heart, tutors at Vulva University say: 'To have good sex we need to let go of the conscious control we normally exercise and let ourselves be open to playing games in a way we might not in normal life. The value in BDSM is often allowing our unexpressed selves to surface.' Orgasm coach Lisa Turner adds that what we don't express consciously (i.e. asking for what we want in life) will be expressed unconsciously so BDSM is a way of asking for what you want within a specific limit or scene.

Dossie Easton and Janet Hardy have written several excellent books about BDSM and ecstasy. They believe that we need to value pleasure and ecstasy as a culture and acknowledge that there is something bigger than ourselves that gives us energy. In *Radical Ecstasy* they say: 'We think that most people feel pretty trapped behind four walls and are pretty desperate to escape from them at least some of the time – we certainly are. We've found that our experiences in getting rid of our walls have left us feeling happier, sexier, stronger, freer, and much more loving (and yes, occasionally kind of scared too, although usually a good kind of scared).'

The connection between pain and pleasure

'BDSM activities introduce two chemicals into the body,' says London Faerie. 'Adrenaline – the 'fight or flight' hormone and endorphins – the body's natural painkiller. By playing with these two chemicals it's possible to make the bottom very high, very quickly. There is also an erotic aspect to this – as the bottom gets more aroused, the body gets flooded with more chemicals and then it all feels even better! It's a win-win.'

'Love, sex, pain and violence all stimulate the release of similar chemicals and hormones in the human body,' says Wendy Strgar, founder and CEO, Good Clean Love. 'Endorphins that are released in painful experiences are often perceived as pleasurable. Stress and pain can also stimulate serotonin and melatonin production in the brain, which transforms painful experiences into pleasure. The release of epinephrine and norepinephrine in pain can also cause a pleasurable "rush". Normal human biological response actually supports the complex and mysterious link between pain and pleasure, which we see in the runner's high and the facial expressions during orgasmic release.' She points out that it's not surprising that the practice of combining painful techniques with sexuality is ancient, and the practice is now known as BDSM.

Sensation play is therefore progressive, can enhance orgasm and lead to altered states of consciousness. Submissives have described leaving their bodies for a short period of time, which is freeing and meditative. As we become more sexually excited our bodies have a higher capacity for pain so the key with any kink play is to start slowly and build tension. 'When we are aroused the line between pain and pleasure is blurred they say, and you may find you are happy to go further and experience things that you never imagined. Your body will be flooded with endorphins, which can radically change your perception of pleasure and pain,' say Klimist and Heart.

Consensuality, negotiation and trust

D/S is a game of negotiation, responsibility and trust. It's not about one person doing something to the other person. It's about mutual pleasure, and you are both there to have a good time. It's therefore important to set limits before you begin. Know what you will and won't do in a scene and to have your safe word if things get too intense. Many people use the traffic light system: 'green' for OK, 'yellow' for slow down and 'red' for stop. It's also important to remember that being submissive in sex games is very different to being submissive in real life, which has negative connotations. To be submissive in sex play requires power – if you don't have power you can't give it away for an agreed period of time. It's also important to play both sides – top and bottom, even if you gravitate towards one or the other. This is so you know what your playmates feel when you play together. Lastly, it's wise to test out any new toys and sensations on yourself first before bringing in a play partner so that you know how they feel and how far to go.

Getting started

Vulva University tutors, Kyree Klimist and Mikaya Heart suggest making a list to begin with:

- Things you like.

- Things you don't like.

- Things you want to try – any fantasies you would like to explore. It's sometimes easier to be more candid on paper so you could email some fantasies to each other.

- A wish list of any pervertibles you'd like to try.

Good Sex tip: **Spray perfume all over your body and blindfold him. When you're near him he'll be able to smell you in advance and it will be a huge turn on.**
Mistress Josephine

Common fantasies

Our top sexual fantasies include rape, voyeurism, power play, exhibitionism, and same sex experiences. Fantasy is a very erotic tool. If you need a bit of inspiration I recommend Anne Rice's *Sleeping Beauty* trilogy, Nancy Friday's *My Secret Garden* and Brett Kahr's *Sex & the Psyche*.

Basic bondage kit

It's easy to spend a small fortune on pervertibles, particularly if you develop a taste for a certain activity and want good quality tools. I like Heartwood Whips – a US cottage industry that makes high quality whips and floggers in varying materials. Floggers are my favourite tool because they are sensual, gorgeous to look at and can be used in lots of different ways. You can find cheaper bits via online sex boutiques such as Love Honey or more high-end pieces at Coco de Mer. As a rule I'd say don't spend too much on a piece of kit unless you're sure you enjoy the activity. Hire a dungeon for an evening and play with the items there or do an educational workshop where equipment is provided so you can test things out first-hand.

Your brain is your biggest piece of kit – imagination – so develop that one in terms of fantasy scenarios. Be creative with household items and check out DIY stores – pegs, ropes, candles; something innocuous like rose thorns that can be used for multiple purposes! Basic pervertibles include floggers, cuffs, rope – cotton, hemp or silk – in various lengths, candles (basic wax or soy – no coloured wax for the first layer, as it burns hotter), blindfold, fetish clothing and shoes, a feather boa or ostrich tickler, massage oils, and safety scissors for the rope.

Trade shows such as the annual Erotica UK are great places to test out larger pieces of kit such as bondage chairs; sex swings and specially made beds.

Practical exercises

At a recent workshop, Faerie mentioned that it's a good idea to start kink play with a concious touch exercise (connecting with blindfolds and one-handed touch). 'This is because all too often you see people hitting a sub/slave without paying enough attention to what they are doing or what impact it is having,' he says. 'BDSM becomes so much more when touch becomes conscious, allowing us to sense energy and feel how close to the edge your bottom is at any given moment.'

- Connect with blindfolds – take it in turns to be top/bottom and lead each other around the room in a dance. Keep it playful and try to sense each other's mood and what is needed. Incorporate the fall and catch exercise.

- Spanking – your hand is just as good as a flogger and more practical, depending on location. Aim for the fleshy bits – buttocks and thighs and start slow and light, gradually building tension. It's good to get into a rhythm and to pace the blows a little to give your lover chance to experience the sensation and afterglow.

- Basic rope bondage – Ava Cadell, sex therapist describes a basic rope tying exercise in her online Loveology course on power play. The idea is to start at the neck (keeping it loose around the neck) and tie a knot every few inches vertically down the front of the body in line with the erogenous zones – nipples and genital area so that the knots rub against these areas when your lover wriggles. When you reach the genitals loop the rope through and take it up their back to the starting point. You then tie another piece of rope horizontally between the first knots to create a diamond shape that can be pulled taut to hold your bottom in place.

I recommend a workshop in rope bondage so you can learn the techniques properly under supervision. Midori's book *The Seductive Art of Japanese Rope Bondage* has gorgeous pictures to illustrate, and I also like the Two Knotty Boys, who have written a book on rope bondage. You'll find their videos showing various techniques on YouTube.

Safety precautions

There are some no-go zones where it's not safe to hit, says Sir Claire Black, a Pro-Domme. Generally fleshy bits are OK but you need to avoid the kidneys, the face, ears, any bony bits, the tailbone, spine, hips, throat and ankles. Be aware that each of us has a pain threshold scale of 1-10 so what works for some will be a turn off for others. Skin sensitivity can also vary hugely during the month depending on where we are in our hormonal cycle and what else is going on. It's not a good idea to play if you're feeling emotional or upset or have been ill because the immune system is compromised. The sensible thing is to practise anything new on yourself first so you know what feels good, and to ask for feedback during a play session.

Fetish sex

Alfred Binet, a French psychologist and hypnotist, introduced the terms 'erotic fetish' and 'sexual fetish' in 1887. He believed they arose as a result of associations – for example, memories from childhood. Most of us have a fetish of one kind or another and they can heighten sex. Wearing a pair of kinky leather boots can give you a power rush and is visually arousing. Common fetishes include clothing, rubber and rubber items, footwear, body parts, leather jackets and items, and soft materials and fabrics. A friend of mine tells me he gets lots of pleasure from his rubber gas mask.

Body modification

Body modification is a term for alteration of body parts for non-medical reasons including aesthetics, a rite of passage, sexual enhancement and self-expression. Most of us have had some kind of piercing – usually the ears, and other types can intensify sensation during arousal – tongue piercings, clitoral piercings, genital beading, scrotal implants, and nipple piercings. Foreskin removal and restoration is also practised. Being pierced or tattooed together is an intimate, ritualistic activity and good to mark a period of change. Done well, tattoos are beautiful pieces of artwork that act a visual reminder of an intention or desire.

Taking it further

I recommend Sacred Pleasures' kink workshops if you're interested in learning specific techniques. I recently did one on fire and wax play with DK and Luisa Leather, which taught me how to safely use firesticks, candles and knives for ritual play. Having a body to practise on makes all the difference and quite a few couples came to learn together. You can also book in for a kinky initiation with Faerie or have one-to-one kinky coaching together. Mistress Josephine, a London-based Pro-Domme has set up The London School of Mistressing, which also runs courses for couples in developing power play.

I find the whole kink scene very educational – it's the ethos behind the leather community and it has a long history in the US. Fetlife (www.fetlife.com) is a free social networking site and you'll find links to local munches and workshops. The main club events include Kinky Salons, Torture Garden, Night of the Senses, Subversion, and Pedestal in London. Erotica UK has an annual erotic ball, which is glamorous and fun.

Bookwise, I recommend Jay Wiseman's *SM101*, which is a fantastic introduction to the basics and safety of SM play. Greenery Press is a small specialist publisher focusing on BDSM.

Summing Up

- BDSM is an acronym for sexual power play incorporating bondage and discipline, sadomasochism, and dominance and submission. It's an alluring area of sexuality because it's a bit edgy, mysterious and risky. It's progressive and can lead to altered states of consciousness and a deeper connection with play partners because it explores sensation play and the connection between erotic pain and pleasure.

- The best way to get started is reading some good introductory books and attending a few workshops to learn different skills and techniques.

Chapter Seven

Orgasm

A brief history

Cleopatra demanded two orgasms a day.

The female orgasm has an intriguing history. Hippocrates (470-410BC) believed that conception happened when male and female sexual fluid merged. The ancient Greeks had an emphasis on sex for pleasure and the word 'orgasmus' means 'to swell with moisture, to be excited and eager'. Greek men were a little bit freaked out at the thought of being used for sex and started tying their women up to keep them under control (funny that nowadays men pay Pro-Dommes to do this).

Sexual repression was prevalent with Christianity hence the missionaries and their disapproval of adventurous sex positions. Raymond L McIlvenna, author of *The Pleasure Quest,* points out that there is nothing in the Bible to say that sex or orgasm was sinful – the opposite in fact; it contains lots of sexual scenes, songs and poetry. For later Christians however, sex became a means of control. In the Middle Ages, (5th century to 15th century) female pleasure was associated with witches and devilry, and chastity and abstinence were advocated.

Clitoral orgasm was acknowledged by the 18th century, but it's only recently that we've found out the clitoral body is much bigger than we thought. In the 19th century, female orgasm or 'hysteria' was thought to be an illness with the symptoms of arousal, erotic fantasy, genital lubrication and general 'irritability'. Maggie Gyllenhall's new film *Hysteria* explores this period of time.

In the 1920s, Freud thought that clitoral orgasms were inferior to 'mature' vaginal ones. Thankfully his opinion was discounted. In the 1960s, Kinsey's sex research brought clitoral pleasures back into focus and the vagina was pretty

'Cleopatra demanded two orgasms a day.'

much ignored until 1981 when the G-spot was so-named in honour of Ernst Gräfenberg's research in the 1940s. Thanks to G-spot pioneers like Deborah Sundahl we now know that women can ejaculate during a G-spot orgasm.

So where are we today? Female orgasm is still a hot topic and the subject of documentaries like Liz Canner's *Orgasm Inc*. It's become high tech, and researchers at Rutgers University are using brain imagery scanning techniques to find out what is happening in the brain when we orgasm. Psychology professor Barry Komisaruk has found that almost every area of the brain is activated at orgasm, and the research aims to find out where the blockage occurs in the 25% of women who rarely or don't have orgasms. Researchers acknowledge that orgasm and sexuality is very complex involving physical, psychological and emotional components. It's an exciting time for the science of orgasm.

The sexual response cycle

In the 1950s, Masters & Johnson defined the sexual response cycle as having four stages – excitement, plateau, orgasm and resolution. By measuring heart and pulse rate and uterine contractions they were able to define the 'average' orgasm in terms of length and found that male orgasm is much shorter – average of 8 seconds compared to female orgasm lasting 20 seconds. They also found that women have multiple orgasms if stimulation continues.

Orgasm and self-pleasure

Statistics show that the more you masturbate the more likely you are to experience orgasm. (source: The Social Organisation of Sexuality, 1994 by Laumann et al). Kinsey's sex research found that 68.2% of men had their first orgasm via masturbation compared to 40% of women. Masturbation is the best way to learn your sexual response and the different types of orgasm. Identify your point of no return and you can learn how to build sexual tension in the body to experience a full body orgasm. We have sex toys to help us come, but I think it's helpful to put them aside once in a while and learn how to orgasm from manual touch. It takes longer but the orgasm feels different – more diffuse – and can be quite intense. Masturbation also helps you to identify how you like to be touched.

66

What to do if you're having a hard time reaching climax? Sexpert, Emily Dubberley suggests the following psychological trick, 'Try tricking your brain by deciding you're banned from reaching orgasm. This can help you get away from thinking too hard about your climax – often one of the best ways to kill it – and leaves you to focus on the sensations you're experiencing – which in turn, will help boost your orgasmic chances.'

The benefits of orgasm

Orgasm coach Dr Lisa Turner explains that they improve our physical health, relax us, release energy blockages, and reduce the health risks of prostate cancer and heart disease. They also make us nicer people to be around. When our sexual energy is flowing properly we are able to connect with people more easily because our flow and heart energy is open. 'Harnessing and transmuting sexual energy improves your vitality and increases feelings of wellbeing. You experience more energy and are more motivated in your daily life. You enjoy your body more including moving your body and exercising.'

Different types of orgasm

- Clitoral – ('the first gate' in tantra). 80% of women say they can't orgasm without clitoral stimulation. Clitoral orgasms stimulate the pudendal nerve system and we now know that all orgasms are clitoral in origin because the clitoris is much bigger that we thought. Have a play with your clitoral hood and see if you can give yourself a mini-erection. It will swell in size when you're aroused. If you can't take direct stimulation then massage around the hood to diffuse the sensation. See if you can bring yourself to climax without any penetration. Men – take note, it's not one size fits all. Clitorises come in different shapes and sizes and locations.

- G-spot ('second gate'). Turner says once this gate is open you'll no longer need clitoral stimulation. To open it try masturbating with a vibrator inside your vagina so you can contract your PC muscle around the shaft. G-spot orgasms feel slightly different – more diffuse and deeper because you are stimulating the pelvic parasympathetic nervous system. Try the Lelo Gigi G-spot massager or the Hitachi Magic Wand, which has a Gee-Whiz silicone G-spot attachment.

- Full body orgasm ('third gate'). Dr Wilhelm Reich, a radical psychoanalyst and contemporary of Freud in the 1920s, discovered this. He believed in the power of orgasm for physical health and developed a theory about 'orgones' or cosmic energy that could prevent illness. He was a little bit ahead of his time with his 'orgasmotherapy' and contemporaries dismissed his theories as nonsense. The aim is to get your sexual energy circulating through your whole body in order to experience a full body orgasm.

How to have a full body orgasm

Orgasms are lovely but they can be quite short, so it's a case of learning how to retain and expand sexual energy so you can experience a longer, stronger climax that makes you tingle from tip to toe. The first step is building strength in your PC muscles by doing regular Kegel exercises – try Jade love eggs or Smart Balls and get into the habit of wearing them when you're out and about. Stronger internal muscles will produce more pleasurable contractions.

The next step, says Dr Turner, is to learn your orgasmic response and focus on retaining sexual energy in your body. The more energy you can hold the bigger your orgasm will be when you let go. This technique involves identifying your point of no return and then stopping all stimulation just before. It's challenging because by this point the sensations feel very pleasurable and it's tempting to keep going. Stop! Repeat the cycle seven times using your breath to draw energy inwards and upwards. If it helps, visualise your orgasm as a colour and imagine it circulating to fill your whole body. On the final cycle (or as near to seven as you can get) let your body dissolve into orgasm.

Turner calls this the 'excruciating pleasure of a full body orgasm' and describes it as an endless wave of pleasure that fills your entire being. One of her students on the energy transmutation course (www.energytransmutation.com) holds the record for an orgasm lasting 23 minutes. 'The secret to good sex has nothing to do with the physical body,' she says. 'It is actually about the emotional and spiritual connection between two people. At orgasm, the ego (lower self) is surrendered. When you know how to exchange your sexual and orgasmic energy you will truly be making love and connecting at a spiritual level. The experience of this goes way beyond any physical pleasure and it is exquisite bliss!' It's sex at soul level and it will strengthen your physical relationship as well as your own health and wellbeing.

Playwork exercises

The first step to improving your orgasms is being mindful and conscious about sex and orgasm.

- Be conscious and present when you next have an orgasm. Visualise it as a colour or shape and imagine it filling your entire consciousness as well as your lover. Create an intention and visualise an outcome you desire. You can use the power of sexual energy in this way to bring about change and transformation in your life. This exercise is about 'creating' love rather than 'making' love and it will change the vibration of sex from being genitally to mentally focused. By radiating love energy you attract more of it to you.

- Try to widen your definition of orgasm and, 'Give yourself permission to stay fully aroused for a long time,' says Mikaya Heart. She points out that we are taught to control our bodies from an early age with potty training, and if we are strong-willed we may have trouble letting go enough to orgasm. 'Good sex is not just about your vulva; it involves every nerve ending in your body, so learn how to touch with awareness. Touch your lover all over and ask him or her to touch you. Most women will come more easily if their whole body is aroused through gentle, light, sensitive stroking.' She suggests spending 15 minutes a day stroking your body in different ways to learn what arouses you and then transferring this to your sex play.

'Be conscious and present when you next have an orgasm.'

Taking it further

There are lots of excellent books out there on the topic of orgasm. I recommend *Urban Tantra* by Barbara Carrelas, Lou Paget's books, Mae West's autobiography in which she talks about harnessing sexual energy, Mantak Chia's books on Taoist sexual practice, the Bodansky's guide to extended massive orgasm, and Easton and Hardy's books on BDSM and orgasm: *Radical Ecstasy* and *The New Topping* and *The New Bottoming* guides.

Summing Up

▪ Master & Johnson's sexual response cycle defines the four stages as excitement, plateau, orgasm and resolution. They defined the average male orgasm as lasting eight seconds compared to 20 seconds in women. Women are also capable of having multiple orgasms if stimulation continues.

▪ There are three types of orgasm – clitoral, G-spot and full body, although all orgasms are now thought to be clitoral in origin. Masturbation is the best way to learn your orgasmic response and the different types of orgasm. It also enables you to build sexual tension in the body so you can experience a full body orgasm and practise sex magic.

▪ BDSM orgasms explore the link between pleasure and pain and have been described as transcendental. Tantra also teaches men how to separate orgasm and ejaculation, and various techniques to enhance orgasm and sexual pleasure.

Chapter Eight

Aphrodisiacs

Food and sex have a long history. The ancient Romans and Greeks knew how to use food for sexual pleasure and enhancement and many of their celebrations involved food. In *The Pleasure Quest,* Raymond McIlvenna points out that they used all manner of potions and lotions as love charms and had an awareness of how body fluids such as sweat and semen could attract a lover. Semen was added to fluids to entice women and giving women an item soaked in male sweat could enhance desire.

Medieval India was also big on food and erotic pleasure. The *Kama Sutra* of Vatsyayana has a section devoted to aphrodisiacs and seduction, which helpfully states that 'should the object of your affection remain distant and all natural avenues of seduction have failed then the pursuer should not hesitate to have recourse to artificial methods'. It lists various lotions and potions to ingest and rub into body organs and provides a list of recipes to keep a man potent into old age: 'a mixture of ghee, sugar, liquorice, mixed with equal quantities of the juice of fennel and milk drunk daily will guarantee the preservation of one's sexual powers well into old age'.

Raymond McIlvenna states that the sequel to the *Kama Sutra* was a 15th century work called *The Ananga Ranga – a Hindu Ritual of Love* by Kalyana Malla. It has a chapter on medicines and aphrodisiacs, including seven recipes for female orgasm, nine recipes to delay male orgasm, eight aphrodisiacs, plus recipes to enlarge his bits and tighten hers.

'The ancient Romans and Greeks knew how to use food for sexual pleasure and enhancement and many of their celebrations involved food.'

What are aphrodisiacs?

Aphrodisiacs are foods, scents or objects that stimulate desire and enhance sexual performance. All food engages our mind and senses but there are certain sexy foods that top the list for boosting libido and desire. 'Aphrodisiacs are said to sexually enhance, increase or improve the status quo of a person's sex drive and performance,' says Dr Ava Cadell. 'Food and sex are two of the greatest pleasures known to mankind and both appetites need to be fulfilled. They are part of our vital life force and stimulate all of our senses.'

She explains that there are different classes of aphrodisiac:

- Psycho-physiological, which include visual foods (phallic or cunic-shaped) that remind us of the body, for example, figs, ginseng, lychees and peaches. This is food that appeals to our tactile, olfactory and aural senses. A psychological aphrodisiac can be a smell that transports you back to a sexy time by stimulating your nervous system.

- Internal – things we imbibe to create a physical response – foods, alcohol, herbs or love potions. The aim of these is to excite the body, increase genital sensitivity and turn us into the Duracell bunny!

Eating as a sensual ritual

Dr Cadell suggests cooking with love, passion and creativity as a way to nourish your relationship on all levels because this will give meals a different vibration. Julie Peasgood, author of *The Greatest Sex Tips in the World,* suggests getting into the habit of cooking lovely light suppers to fuel you both for sex in the evening. Finger foods such as sushi and sashimi are good because you can eat them on the floor or in the bedroom. I went to a Sensual Soiree tantra evening once and was blindfolded and fed dessert by several men. I couldn't see them or what I was eating but the experience was erotic because the food was being fed to me in creative ways. We learned to slow right down, and how to use our bodies to feed each other as well as our hands.

Fasting to heighten your senses

In *The Sex Book*, Suzi Godson suggests doing a 30-hour advance fasting pre sexy weekend, which includes abstinence and chastity to heighten your senses and help you detox. This will make the food (and each other) taste sweeter when you do finally succumb. Here's her recipe:

- On the Thursday before have juice, fruit, water and herbal teas only, to detox. Eating bland food the day before play will put your sensory system on overdrive and make your body more responsive. Buy lots of finger foods such as sashimi, oysters, asparagus, caviar, gravlax, blinis and plenty of fruits – strawberries, mango, cherries and ice cream. Serve with ice-cold white wine or champers. Take it in turns to feed each other and use a blindfold to heighten taste and sensation.

We are what we eat, so whatever you consume your body fluids will taste of. Eat plenty of fruit and drink water to hydrate your body so that you taste sweeter. A drop of champers on the labia or tip of his penis feels bubbly and tastes sweet. No-nos before oral sex include beer, curry and asparagus for him. Raw coconut oil is great rubbed into skin as well as for use in food.

Dine off each other's bodies Japanese-style or for a little impromptu fun try sploshing – a food fight. Protective sheeting comes in useful here. There's a very funny scene in the *Belle de Jour* TV series when Belle is asked to indulge in a bit of sploshing by a kinky client. Her initial resistance: 'My hair!' 'My kitchen!' is soon forgotten and she gets into the swing of it. There's something to be said for being silly and losing your inhibitions around food and proper table dining customs.

'Dine off each other's bodies Japanese-style or for a little impromptu fun try sploshing – a food fight.'

Top 20 coital foods

Here's a list of 20 sexy foods as recommended by psychetruth.com and Dr Ava Cadell. They contain a wealth of vitamins and minerals – the cornerstones for sexual health being vitamins C, E, B6, potassium and zinc. There's nothing outrageously expensive or hard to find here – with the exception of oysters and truffles maybe. Nothing that a day trip to a French market won't sort out.

Oysters

Caviar, shellfish and oysters are all high in zinc, which helps sperm production and motility. One oyster contains 12mg of zinc, a significant boost to the average daily intake of 8mg. Seafoods were thought to be aphrodisiacs because they are linked to Aphrodite, goddess of love and sex, who came from the sea – and the testicles of Uranus, apparently. Oysters look and feel like vulvas so can be fun to play with. There are at least 15 varieties, so if you've tried one and didn't like it try another variety.

Celery

Phallic in appearance, celery is a fun finger food served with dips. It boosts blood circulation and produces male hormone pheromones that help to attract women.

Almonds

Are high in zinc and also a pheromone stimulator. They contain essential fatty acids and amino acids, which help us to enjoy sex.

Asparagus

High in vitamin E for sperm production and also contains phosphorus and calcium. It helps the body to produce sex hormones and provides a slow energy release so we have more stamina. Studies indicate that it can help men and women to orgasm, although I'd say never swallow if he's been eating asparagus. It has a very strong flavour, which makes semen taste bitter!

Figs

Adam and Eve covered their genitals with a fig leaf and they have a long history of use as an aphrodisiac. They look like mini vaginas, smell sweet and musky and contain seeds which are very good for you. They help to increase sperm production and motility and provide a slow release of energy so it's helpful to keep a few dried figs in your bag to nibble during the day.

Watermelon

It's juicy, cool and tastes fabulous and it's also packed with vitamins A, B, C, beta-carotene, potassium and electrolytes. It also has the highest lycopene content of all fruit and veg. It supports prostate and erectile function and makes semen and vaginal juices taste sweet.

Garlic

Garlic boosts circulation and thins the blood, meaning you'll be aroused and lubricated that much quicker. It is also antiviral and anti-inflammatory so helps ward off colds and coughs. However, you need to eat it together otherwise the smell and taste is an anaphrodisiac.

Bananas

Bananas are packed with vitamins, fibre and potassium to help sex hormone production and release. They provide a slow release of energy so can combat that mid-afternoon slump and ensure you have energy in the evening.

Pine nuts

Pine nuts have a long history of use as an aphrodisiac. They contain vitamins, minerals, fatty acids, amino acids and zinc. Add to pesto or toast them and toss over your coital salad says dietician Elizabeth Brown – see her recipe on YouTube for a sexy salad made from rocket, pine nuts, fruit nipples and dark chocolate.

Tomatoes

Also known as 'love apples' and linked to matters of the heart. Cut them in half and they resemble the chambers of the heart. Red, cunic and juicy, they contain high amounts of lycopene.

Chocolate

Casanova was addicted to it. It has a long history of use as a sexual stimulant by the Peruvian Indians and Montezuma, who drank 50 cups a day to give him the energy to service his harem of 600 women. Chocolate contains chemicals that help the body to release serotonin and dopamine, replicating how we feel when we're in love. Theobromine boosts energy levels and arginine is an amino acid, which improves blood circulation. Go for good quality chocolate – the darker the better for a bigger cocoa hit. Raw chocolate is the ultimate aphrodisiac and much tastier. Nutritionist Fiona Corliss recommends a couple of squares first thing in the morning to pep up your energy levels and boost libido.

Avocados

'Casanova was addicted to chocolate!'

Slice them in half and they look like a womb. Dr Ava Cadell points out that it takes nine months for an avocado to blossom, which is rather apt in human life terms. The Mayans and Aztecs used them as a sex booster and they contain vitamin B6, potassium, and omegas 3 and 6, so are good for hormonal balance. On the tree they resemble two testicles so go by the nickname 'testicle tree'. They also taste great dipped in balsamic vinegar.

Spices

Studies show that nutmeg, cinnamon and clove induce sexual excitement and enhance arousal and pleasure. Alan Hirsch, developer of the Smell & Taste Treatment and Research Foundation in Chicago has published research, which shows that popular aphrodisiac scents include cinnamon, vanilla, lavender and pumpkin pie spice. Ginger helps maintain a healthy immune system and boosts circulation so will warm you up as well as quicken arousal. Studies show that having warm feet (wearing socks!) is essential for orgasm so a cup of ginger tea will help there.

Caffeine

Coffee is a good pick-me-up and in low doses acts as an orgasm and desire enhancer. Too much will have the opposite effect though, lowering sensitivity and impairing his erection. Coffee and chocolate – mocha – is a good combination.

Alcohol

A social lubricant and our most commonly used aphrodisiac; it has long been celebrated in poetry and song, says Raymond McIlvenna, as the intoxicating effects of 'wine, women and song'. In small quantities alcohol relaxes us, lowers inhibitions and reduces anxiety. It also delays ejaculation so can help him to last for longer. However, too much can impair semen production and performance by anaesthetising the penis, making erection difficult. In women it leads to a slower and less intense orgasm. So, it's a bit of a double-edged sword. It boosts desire but can impair performance, and beer goggles are never a good idea.

Rocket (Aragula)

It's been used as an aphrodisiac since Roman times. Contains vitamin C and potassium for hydration and helps with sex hormone function and secretion. Good for the coital salad.

Liquorice root

It's dark and phallic in appearance and apparently capable of bringing on lustful urges by helping oxygen to move to the genital area 40% faster, according to research. Handy for the glove box, then.

Oats (Avena sativa)

Oats contain the most protein of all the cereal grains, polyunsaturated fats and are low GI and highly digestible. 'Sowing your oats' is a common term that refers to a man spreading his seed and it has some truth in it. Studies at the Advanced Institute of Human Sexuality on a pure extract of Avena sativa in powder form found that oats have a positive effect on male and female sex hormones. They increase free testosterone in the blood, which boosts male libido. The extract is also high in flavonoids, which are linked to our sex hormone activity. Raymond McIlvenna, author of *The Pleasure Quest* says they've had a positive effect on his own sex drive (as a 67-year-old at the time of writing his book). Study participants reported more sexual thoughts, fantasies, lubrication and sensation during sex. Go to work on a bowl of porridge.

Honey (moon)

Greek and Roman estates often had beehives and the Romans offered their god Priapus a honey and milk drink as an aphrodisiac. It is also described as a cure for impotence in the ancient text *The Perfumed Garden*. Bee pollen is highly concentrated and incredibly good for us. Choose raw honey as it has a higher nutritional value.

Eggs

Eggs are cunic-shaped and were considered to be an aphrodisiac by ancient Greeks and Egyptians, who thought that god created them out of the sun and moon. Aphrodite called sparrow eggs 'birds of love'. They symbolise new life and fertility and the French still believe in the tradition of breaking an egg on the doorstep to create a large family. Caviar or 'pearls of the sea' as they are known, are the ultimate aphrodisiac. Caviar takes its name from the Persian word 'Khav-yar' which means 'cake of strength'. They are full of protein and zinc, which are essential for testosterone production and libido.

The Orgasmic Diet

The Orgasmic Diet is a book by Marrena Lindberg that explores the link between diet, orgasms and PC exercises. Lindberg did considerable research into aphrodisiac foods and created her own diet plan based on this to improve her orgasms and sexual response. It's not a diet, thankfully, and includes dark chocolate, a high quantity of fish oils to aid blood flow and genital response, and protein-rich foods. This, in combination with regular pelvic toning exercises (Lindberg recommends the Gyneflex) can give you very strong orgasms and a high libido. I enjoyed the book and there are lots of Internet testimonials from happy participants.

Sex herbs

Sex herbs can increase libido and enhance sexual response and orgasms. They're also fun to test out with a lover. I recommend buying them in a decent strength from a reputable pharmacy such as Tree People, Victoria Health, or Detox Your World. The main ones are muira puama, maca, damiana, saw palmetto, Avena sativa (wild oat herb), dong quai, ashwanga, horny goat weed, ginseng, gingko biloba, and yohimbe.

Dr Michel Jemec, a Swiss gynaecologist who is studying the link between libido and LH hormone, suggests having maca parties to improve libido, as it has an LH type effect on the body, boosting energy. I've had good results with maca and add it to desserts or make a sexy smoothie with milk, banana, honey and cinnamon.

Pheromones

Pheromones are hormonal substances secreted in the body of humans, animals, insects and plants to attract the opposite sex. The concept has been around since ancient times. The ancients used body secretions in potions to attract a lover (try dabbing your vaginal juices on your neck and watch the effect on men). It's an exciting area of scientific research and a 2002 study at San Francisco State University found that synthetic pheromones in women's perfume increased intimate contact with men.

'Pheromones are hormonal substances secreted in the body of humans, animals, insects and plants to attract the opposite sex.'

There are a few pheromone perfumes on the market. I recently bought a bottle of Escentric Molecules: Molecule 01 from Coco de Mer. Sam Roddick tells me the effect is potent – she's had staff followed home, and apparently Naomi Campbell has ordered a box of it! So far I've had lots of compliments when wearing it, which is odd as I can't smell it but it must be doing something to bring out my natural pheromones!

Summing Up

- Food and sex have a long history and certain foods can enhance sexual arousal and desire. Most healthy foods are good for libido as they contain vitamins and nutrients that nourish sexual function. Aphrodisiacs contain a wealth of vitamins and minerals – the cornerstones for sexual health being vitamins C, E, B6, potassium and zinc.

- Be creative with your cooking and explore YouTube, as there are many videos featuring aphrodisiac foods and recipes. Combine good food with exercise, PC exercise and rest, and you'll notice an improvement in your libido. Alcohol is our most popular aphrodisiac and is fine in moderation – lowering inhibitions and relaxing us. Red wine opens blood vessels so can aid circulation to the genitals. Champagne gives us a heady high and the bubbles feel decadent on the body, and sweet dessert wines also have a reputation as a sexual enhancer.

- Book a couples' cookery holiday such as www.cookinfrance.com, which is a top cookery school run by celebrity chef Jim Fisher and his wife Lucy. Jim credits his long and happy marriage of 29 years to the fact that he and Lucy cook together and says he's observed many relationships being recharged through a cookery holiday at his school. They offer a course called *Cooking as Foreplay - Beyond Aphrodisiacs*, which is designed for couples of all ages.

Chapter Nine

Common Problems

Sexual problems are more common than you think . . .

Male sexual dysfunction

This is defined as erectile dysfunction (impotence), premature ejaculation, delayed ejaculation, painful sex and loss of libido. Dr John Tomlinson of the Sexual Advice Association says it is more common than we realise, affecting 7-8% of men aged 20-40, 11% of men over 60 and over half of men over 70.

Female sexual dysfunction

Female sexual dysfunction (FSD) is now a recognised medical syndrome identified as loss of sexual desire and arousal, problems with orgasm, and painful sex. According to a 1999 study reported in the Journal of the American Medical Association (JAMA), it affects 43% of women. This study was controversial as it only included 1,500 women. There were also concerns that drug companies sponsored the research and that 'FSD' is a marketing term designed to sell more drugs to women.

The Australian medical journalist Ray Moynihan wrote about this recently in the British Medical Journal saying that FSD is a complicated issue and requires holistic treatment. So far, efforts to create a female Viagra haven't worked because a woman's sexual response is more complicated. Liz Canner's documentary *Orgasm Inc* talks about FSD in detail if you want some background to the studies.

I shudder at the word 'dysfunction' but as Suzi Godson points out, women do have sex issues and will benefit from physical and psychological treatment. She says if the drug companies don't fund the research then who will?

In 2002, the Datamonitor Group did a follow-up and found that almost half of women suffer from sexual problems but less than half seek help. This is a concern because it shows that many of us are putting up with a sub-standard sex life. We live in a sexualised society and there is pressure to have great sex daily, but many of us still don't talk about sex either because we're embarrassed or because we don't want to upset our lovers.

'The Kinsey Institute is also due to publish a survey this year that suggests women today are having less sex than their grandmothers.'

(Source: Psychologies, July 2011).

Drugs may be helpful in some circumstances but a holistic approach incorporating diet and lifestyle changes, self-help, psychosexual therapy and couples' counselling will work for most. The first step is to find out if the problem is a result of a hormonal imbalance such as low testosterone or falling estrogen levels.

Here's an overview of the most common problems and what to do about them.

For her:

Loss of libido ('Lib' – 'Libet' in Latin = 'to want or desire')

According to recent media reports, our libidos are at an all-time low. Relate reported a 240% increase in couples attending counselling for loss of desire between 1996 and 2002. The Kinsey Institute is also due to publish a survey this year that suggests women today are having less sex than their grandmothers. (Source: Psychologies, July 2011).

Around a third of us have a low libido and it can happen at certain times of your life (after childbirth, illness or menopause) or be a chronic problem. Symptoms include having no desire to initiate sex, not being receptive to touch, and an absence of thoughts and fantasies about sex. Recent research at Wayne State University in Detroit surveyed the brain activity of women with low libido and found it differed from women with a 'normal' libido – i.e. they didn't experience the same rush of blood to the brain when watching porn and so further research needs to be done.

84

Physical reasons include hormonal imbalances (loss of testosterone), surgery, medication, and medical conditions such as diabetes, thyroid problems, heart disease, MS and depression. Your choice of contraception can also have an impact. My libido nosedived when I started taking the pill and I felt depressed and tearful so decided to stop taking it and find a non-hormonal alternative.

Tiredness, stress, anxiety, poor body image, relationship issues and overusing drugs and alcohol will also have an impact, and this is something counselling can help with. Many of us get bored with our sex lives from time to time, especially in a long-term relationship so it's essential to take a break once in a while and do things differently. Try to remove yourself from your usual domestic set-up and take time out so you can focus on one another rather than the domestics.

Try and pinpoint any triggers. See your GP to find out if your sex hormones (testosterone, LH luteinising hormone and estrogen) are within normal levels. Your hormones change throughout life and your sex drive will dip and rise accordingly. Many women report that they feel more sexual during pregnancy or after menopause, for example. After menopause the body still continues to produce testosterone, which may boost your sex drive.

Professor John Studd who heads the London PMS and Menopause Clinic has lots to say on the topic of female libido. He describes FSD to his patients in terms of changes to 'heart, head and hormones'. 'It is easy to increase the libido by hormonal therapy and apart from the obvious increase in sexual events, such as fantasies, both intercourse, masturbation and orgasms, there is also the knock-on effect that women are happier and have more energy and give out an aura of being sexually confident. Women speak of the extra advantages that attend an improvement in the libido, particularly their enthusiasm for life, self-confidence at work, and a greater feeling of friendship with their partner.'

Dr Elizabeth Vliet has written two books about hormones and sexuality, which explain the impact of loss of testosterone on our sex drive: *It's My Ovaries, Stupid* and *The Savvy Woman's Guide to Testosterone*. She also has a radio talk show called *It's not all in your head – hormones and sex drive*.

Once you've explored any physical reasons, it's helpful to speak to a psychosexual therapist or counsellor about the emotional side of things. You can do this alone but it's good to involve your lover so you can work on things together, says relationship counsellor Marian O'Connor. Cognitive behavioural therapy (CBT) can also be useful as it helps you to change negative thought processes. Contact the Institute of Psychosexual Medicine, College of Sexual and Relationship Therapy, or Relate. You could also take a look at *Cognitive Behavioural Therapy - The Essential Guide*, Need2Know.

Start your own pillow book to note down any day-to-day events: thoughts, fantasies or comments that turn you on. Keep yourself open to sensual opportunities and you'll be surprised at the sense of momentum and energy that builds.

Orgasm problems (Anorgasmia)

This is split into two types:

- Primary anorgasmia is when a woman has never had an orgasm.

- Secondary anorgasmia is when she's had them before but isn't currently.

Physical reasons include lack of foreplay or poor technique, medical conditions that affect the supply of blood to the nerves and clitoris, and weak PC muscles (post-childbirth for example). Psychological reasons include poor sexual communication, relationship difficulties, depression, and not feeling able to relax and 'let go' sexually. Sex therapy can help here.

One thing to remember is that only 70% of women orgasm via penetrative sex. The clitoris is not in a particularly convenient location for penetration so you're more likely to experience orgasm through oral sex, and masturbation with a strong vibrator. You can also try the coital alignment technique (CAT).

I had my first orgasm through masturbation, which took ages and probably contributed to my RSI! I'm glad I didn't give up though, as it was a revelation when it happened and I was very proud of myself. It's easier and far quicker to use a vibrator but I think it's nice to put the toys away sometimes and go back to basics because it's easy to forget you like to be touched. It's also a turn on for your lover to watch you play.

Have a warm bath with aphrodisiac essential oils (ylang-ylang, rose or jasmine) and go to bed with a book of erotica. This will make the self-pleasuring easier because you'll already be turned on. Apply some lubricant and slowly circle your clitoris until you start to feel turned on. Keep the rhythm slow and steady and work out what type of touch feels best until the pressure starts to build. It can take ages but keep going and you will orgasm. Relax your jaw muscles and tongue. Studies have found that wearing socks in bed can help you to orgasm so bear that in mind!

I have strengthened my orgasms by doing PC exercises and making some dietary changes (introducing fish oils and a multivitamin supplement as per *The Orgasmic Diet*). The fish oils improve blood circulation to the brain and genital area so my sexual response and lubrication is much quicker. A strong PC muscle makes uterine contractions much more powerful.

Painful sex (Dyspareunia)

Painful sex is a common problem. Try to determine the source of the pain and get it checked out at your local family planning clinic. Is it superficial i.e. on the labia, clitoris or vaginal entrance, or a deeper pain inside the vagina when you have sex?

Superficial pain can be caused by lack of foreplay or lubrication, or vaginal infections or STIs such as genital warts. Vulvitis is when the vulva becomes inflamed often through excessive washing or bubble baths. Vulvodynia is when the labia are too sensitive to touch. It's also possible to bruise the clitoris through excessive friction but this will usually disappear within a week or so.

Deeper pain can be a sign of cervix problems, which are triggered through deep penetration and womb problems such as fibroids, endometriosis, ovarian cysts, or pelvic inflammatory disease.

At certain times the vagina can be drier – when breastfeeding or taking the pill for example, so bear this in mind and adjust your contraception if necessary. Some tampon brands can also strip the vagina of its natural moisture levels. Try an all-cotton brand such as Natracare.

Sex and the menopause

Painful sex at menopause is common and goes by the charming name of 'atrophic vaginitis'.

One survey found that 84% of menopausal women find sex painful and three quarters said that their relationship had suffered because of it. A fall in estrogen levels makes the vaginal tissues thinner and they produce less natural lubrication. Using localised estrogen (a vaginal ring, cream or pessary) will sort it out or try an organic lubricant such as Yes water-based. Adapt the type of sex you are having so that the woman is in control of the depth of penetration – woman on top and spooning are good positions to try. Spend extra time on foreplay, as rushed sex can be painful for a woman if her vagina is too dry.

Holistic nutritionist Marilyn Glenville has a wealth of information on diet and menopause on her website and has written several excellent books on the topic.

I would also avoid strong washing powders, shower gels and soaps, as they will dry out the vagina. Work on treating any other symptoms (hot flushes) so that your energy levels are higher and you'll be more responsive to touch in general.

Vaginismus

This is when the vaginal muscles go into spasm when you try to have sex, a gynaecological examination or use a tampon. The following medical definition is a bit of mouthful: '[Vaginismus is] the recurrent or persistent involuntary contraction of the perineal muscles surrounding the outer third of the vagina' and 'spasm of the muscles that surround the vagina, causing occlusion of the vaginal opening, so that penile entry is either impossible or painful'.

I experienced this in my teens and 20s and found it very distressing, as I had no idea what was happening. I tried to use tampons but my body seemed to go into shock and I felt sick and shaky every time so abandoned the idea. I avoided having cervical smears and internal examinations for a while because I found them so traumatic. The frustrating thing was that when it came to sex it didn't matter how turned on I was, my body would not relax enough to let a man penetrate me.

I did a lot of reading on the subject and spoke to a girlfriend who had a similar issue (painful sex) and eventually started sex therapy. Masturbation helped and the therapist advised using vaginal trainers (four plastic cones in graduated sizes) so that my body would get used to the sensation. Lots of lubricant, time and patience and it worked. With sex, the key is to wait until you are turned on, use lots of lubricant and gently guide your partner's penis inside you so that you are in control of the depth of penetration. When I have a smear test I put the speculum in myself. Sex therapy helped, as it made me think about my attitudes towards my body and sex in general.

I also recommend doing yoga, as it will relax and open the pelvic area. Regular practice will make a big difference.

Vaginismus is a psychological problem triggered by feelings and thoughts about your body and sexuality. A woman might think her vagina is too small, she's unattractive, or have experienced sexual trauma through childbirth. In the 1960s, sex researchers Masters & Johnson pioneered a technique they called 'Sensate Focus', which involved couples focusing on sensual touch before building up to gentle penetration with a finger and then intercourse. Their studies were successful and the technique is still used in sex therapy today.

For him:

Erectile dysfunction (Impotence)

Erectile dysfunction affects 1 in 10 men (2.3 million men in the UK) according to the Sexual Advice Association. In 75% of cases, it is the result of a physical condition, such as hidden diabetes, high blood pressure, cholesterol or heart disease. This causes the small arteries in the penis (1-2mm width compared to 10mm in the heart area) to clog up so it's more difficult to stay erect. It can also happen when a man is with a new partner and feeling nervous about sex.

As men age their testosterone level naturally falls and this can affect libido, energy and erections. Men over 55 will have less firm erections, produce a smaller amount of semen and have a less intense ejaculation and longer recovery period. Some medications can also have an adverse effect – anti-depressants, Prozac, antibiotics or drugs for high blood pressure.

A blood test at the doctors should reveal any physical problems and the doctor will ask about diet, exercise and lifestyle habits. Smoking restricts blood flow to the penis, stress can prevent erections, and being overweight can lead to high cholesterol and blood pressure.

'Vaginismus is a psychological problem triggered by feelings and thoughts about your body and sexuality.'

Treatments for ED include oral drugs – PDE 5 inhibitors such as Viagra, Cialis, MUSE, Levitra and Imprima, which trap blood in the penis to give him an erection. However, Viagra will only work if he is able to get an erection in the first place! There's also an injection that he can self-administer before sex, and a small pellet, which is inserted into the urethra. He could also try vacuum pumps and testosterone treatment.

The British Society for Sexual Impotence Research is a good starting point for information. The health website NetDoctor (see the help list) has some peer-reviewed articles about ED and other sexual issues.

Premature ejaculation

This is when a man ejaculates shortly after penetration. It's a frustrating problem and affects more than 40% of men according to the Sexual Advice Association, particularly younger men. Dr John Tomlinson says it is connected to sensitivity of the nervous system. In older men it is linked to changes in the prostate gland, a hardening of the arteries, diabetes or a neurological disorder. It can also be caused by stress or anxiety and linked to masturbatory habits as a teenager. If a man taught his body to come too quickly he will continue to ejaculate in the same way.

Fortunately PE is easy to treat and a man can learn how to delay ejaculation so that he and his partner can enjoy sex for longer. Tantric sex explores various techniques to help men separate orgasm and ejaculation. Using a condom can also help as it reduces sensation in the penis.

Sex therapists at COSRT recommend the following techniques:

The Stop/Start Technique (for him)

Set aside half an hour a day to do this exercise. Stimulate yourself manually or ask your lover to do it until you reach the point of no return. Stop stimulation until the feelings subside. Repeat this process a few times before you allow yourself to come. You can then repeat the process when you are inside your partner, varying your thrusts from slow to fast, shallow and deep, to try and regain control of your orgasm. This can be incredibly exciting for your partner as it builds momentum and sexual energy.

The Squeeze Technique (for her)

Put your middle and index fingers below the head of his penis or at the base with your thumb behind his penis and squeeze firmly for four seconds just before he feels he's about to come. Doing this several times stops the urgent need to ejaculate.

Delay sprays reduce the sensation on the glans of the penis so that it takes him longer to come, but some men say they can reduce sensitivity.

Painful sex

Sex can sometimes be painful for a man too if his foreskin is too tight or your vagina feels too tight. Extra lubricant will help. Eczema, psoriasis, STIs, thrush and Peyronie's disease can also cause problems (this is a condition that causes the penis to bend).

Summing Up

■ Most of us experience problems with sex at some point in life. The race is on to develop a female Viagra that will boost female sex drive, but so far nothing has been as effective because our sex drive is more complicated. A combination of physical, psychological, holistic and self-care will work for most women. It's important to get your sex hormone levels checked to make sure you are not deficient, as this will have an impact on your libido and energy levels in general.

■ Your sex drive will ebb and flow at certain times of your life so accept this and try not to worry as it will pick up again. Keep communicating and find other ways to maintain intimacy if you don't feel like having penetrative sex – be inventive. When sex is off the menu it forces us to expand our sexual repertoire.

■ Exercise really is the best foreplay! Keep yourself in the best possible shape as this will feed your libido and make your sexual response that much quicker. Yoga is fantastic for flexibility and tango dancing has proven health benefits for sex drive.

■ Well Man and Well Woman clinics (see your GP or local hospital) will advise on gynaecological or prostate problems, smear tests, contraception and erectile dysfunction. They are also a good source of support if there are any sexual health issues you need advice on.

Chapter Ten

Sexual Health

Making sex as safe as possible means you can relax and enjoy it. There's no drama or worry about unwanted pregnancy or STIs – which can be a concern if you're exploring non-monogamy and open relationships. Regular sexual health checks are vital if you have more than one sexual partner, and are free on the NHS in the UK. Recent statistics have shown a rise in the number of STIs amongst older couples, post-divorce who are likely to be dating again and possibly experimenting with casual sex and swinging. All sexual activities carry a risk – oral sex, rimming, kissing, intercourse and anal sex, but you can minimise it by using condoms, dental dams and having regular STI checks.

Safe sex barriers

Latex condoms

Most men moan about lack of sensitivity when using condoms, but there are tons of brands on the market and the technology is constantly being improved. I've read good reports about Kimono Microthins, a Japanese brand that are skin-like and have no odour or taste. Adding a drop of water-based lube to the tip before he puts it on will also transmit more sensation and help prevent tearing. Always change condoms if you are having vaginal and anal sex as bacteria can be transmitted from the anus to vagina and cause infection. Ditto for any sex toys that are being shared or used for vaginal and anal penetration. A girlfriend of mine tells me it drives men wild when she puts on a condom with her mouth – it increases anticipation, adds oral sensation to the mix and looks very sexy!

'Making sex as safe as possible means you can relax and enjoy it.'

Dental dams

These are designed as a barrier for oral sex and analingus. Oral sex can transmit STIs such as herpes, gonorrhoea, syphilis and chlamydia, and pre-cum can contain STIs and HIV. Glyde dental dams are recommended and you can buy them online from sex boutiques. You can also cut a condom in half to make a makeshift dam. Sexual health experts recommend not brushing your teeth for an hour before unprotected oral sex as tiny abrasions in the mouth can transmit an infection. 'When rimming, make sure that you use a dental dam,' says sexpert, Emily Dubberley. 'Otherwise you're not only risking sexually transmitted infections but also diseases including E.coli. No matter how thoroughly someone washes you can't guarantee that they'll be able to wash away every single germ.'

Latex gloves

Short, filed nails are a must for anal and P-spot play, as the anus is delicate and easy to tear. Using latex gloves makes it easier, more pleasurable and hygienic. Lube them up and off you go. They're also fun for your medical bag as part of fetish play fantasies. Sh! Womenstore sells nice black latex ones, which look just the part.

Lubricants

Lubes have advanced significantly since the days of K-Y Jelly and now come in various flavours, textures and styles. They are a must for all pleasure chests because they're versatile and the best sex is slippery and sensual. Lubes come in three types:

- Water-based – fine for most sex play and compatible with sex toys and condoms. It tends to dry out and needs to be replenished but it feels the most natural.

- Oil-based – lasts longer but isn't condom compatible.

- Silicone – lasts forever, good for anal play and underwater sex. It can be sticky and hard to wash off. Cover any silicone toys with a condom before using silicone lube, as it will rot the material.

Maximus and Pink are two popular brands for anal play and I recommend Yes for all-purpose use, as it's organic and feels fabulous on the skin. I like to know what's in the products I'm using intimately because the mucous membranes of the vagina absorb chemicals much more rapidly than skin. Whatever you put on your bits will end up in the bloodstream and it's not acceptable that some manufacturers don't label the packaging to show a list of ingredients. Pat Thomas wrote an article about this for *The Ecologist* called *'Behind the Label – K-Y Jelly,'* which you can read online. She explains that some lubes contain preservatives such as sodium hydroxide, which can irritate the skin, parabens, which are estrogenic, and glycerine, which contains sugar and is toxic to sperm. It can upset vaginal pH leading to outbreaks of thrush. Studies have also found that some lubricants can affect sperm motility and function, which is a problem if you're trying to get pregnant.

Yes is an organic, natural lube that actually feels like it's good for your skin. It comes in water-based and oil-based, which tastes slightly chocolatey. There are lots of organic brands on the market so shop around and test out a few. Most sell trial-sized sachets, which are ideal for travel.

Sex toys and phthalates

'Toxic sex toys get a red flag' was a recent headline in *The Independent* newspaper. It relates to the use of phthalates, a chemical family that softens sex toys and makes them more pliable. Phthalates are made from phthalic acid, which has been in use since the 1920s and can be found in all types of products including perfume, pesticides and medical devices. Cory Silverberg, About.com's sexuality guide, points out that there is a potential risk but the research is in fledgling stages. He explains that a growing body of research suggests phthalates may have a toxic effect on the male reproductive system, as they mimic oestrogen, leading to lower quality sperm. The effect may be accumulative (as with lube – we don't know what the health implications are for long-term use of certain chemicals). Phthalates have been banned from children's toys but are still used in some adult toys.

Good sex tip: Get organised and pack a bag of pervertibles for any impromptu trips, dirty weekends away, club nights or parties. If you can grab it and go you can be more spontaneous as the safe sex is taken care of. Essential items include a toothbrush, spare pair of knickers, condoms, dam, lube, latex gloves, and your favourite toys and lingerie.

A Danish Environmental Protection Agency report entitled *Survey & Health Assessment of Chemical Substances in Sex Toys* concluded that using sex toys containing phthalates for an hour a day isn't a health risk unless you are pregnant or nursing. However, we don't know what the accumulative effects are, so in my opinion it's wise to avoid phthalates. Fortunately, there are many good quality sex toys on the market that don't contain phthalates and most reputable erotic boutiques have stopped selling them.

Contraception

For full information on all 15 types of contraception I recommend the FPA (Family Planning Association) website (see the help list). It has a contraceptive tool so you can assess which type of contraception suits you and whether it's time for a change. If you've been on the same type of contraception for years it probably is! What suited you in your 20s isn't necessarily the best fit for your 30s and beyond. NHS Choices and NetDoctor also have useful information written by medical professionals, and there's an excellent book called *Contraception – Your Questions Answered* by John Guillebaud. It's presented as a Q&A between a GP and reproductive health-care professional and chapters conclude with common questions asked by patients.

I'm a big fan of natural family planning and use the Persona electronic device to monitor my fertile days. NFP is non-hormonal so doesn't affect your libido and puts a woman in control of her cycle. It's not a barrier device so isn't suitable for casual sex but it works well in a long-term relationship. The basis of it is learning your menstrual cycle and being aware of the fertile times (7 days mid-cycle when you ovulate) so you know when it's safe to have unprotected sex. An egg survives for one day and sperm can live for 5-7 days (most die long before this) so that's why you need to use protection for a week. Knowing your fertility cycle is empowering and means you don't have to put up with the side effects of a form of contraception that doesn't make you happy.

Your local sexual health clinic will put you in touch with an NFP teacher in your area and you can also learn it online via the Billings Method website (www. billingsmethod.com).

Good Sex tip: **Whatever type of contraception you choose make sure you talk about it and review it regularly. It's easy for resentment to build on her side if she feels she's shouldering the responsibility (and side effects) of a hormonal form of contraception. Switch contraception every now and then so you both share the responsibility.**

Summing Up

* All sexual activities carry a risk – oral sex, rimming, kissing, intercourse and anal sex, but you can minimise it by using condoms, dental dams and having regular STI checks.

* Safe sex barriers include condoms, latex gloves and dental dams. Lubricant is the number one sex toy and makes all sexual activity feel more pleasurable. Choose an organic brand to minimise the effects on your sexual health. Some lubes contain undesirable ingredients, so gen up on what's what, and the potential impact on your health.

* There are 15 types of contraception so review it regularly. Natural family planning is the sexiest form of contraception because it's non-hormonal, you can chart it together, and there are no side effects. It takes a bit of time to learn and practise but the effort is worth it.

Chapter Eleven

The Good Sex Survey

Earlier this year we ran a survey to gauge your thoughts on good sex, libido, monogamy, and body image. Here's what you had to say.

What does good sex mean to you?

'Not doing it when I'm too tired. Ideally in the daytime! Actually prioritising it as something that's just as important as going to work, brushing our teeth, putting out the rubbish! So not just a late-night fumble if we still have the energy.'

'An orgasm is always good, but for really good sex I think variety, trying new things and being with a partner you love is important.'

'Uninhibited fun, trust, passion, silly, freedom, exhaustion, exhilaration.'

'My wife and I both enjoy sex and look forward to it on a regular basis. We're both active in sports, which apparently boosts sex drive.'

'A lot! Helps me to feel connected to myself, to feel appreciated, to be able to share myself with another and feel alive.'

'Everything! Good sex with my partner is more than just sex – it validates the desire, passion and love in the partnership.'

'It means whatever type of sex my wife and I decide to have on a given day. It varies. We're very in tune with what the other likes so (almost) all of our sex is good sex.'

'Having a partner who is intuitive and responsive to my sexual needs and preferences, and who can bring me to an amazing climax.'

'Open communication is an essential part of good sex. Sex needs to be varied: sometimes it might be gentle and sensual and sometimes it might be vigorous and active. It's always "doing" sex in the same way that leads to deadness and difficulty in maintaining good sex in a long-term relationship.'

'Sex doesn't always have to be a marathon. Make sure to have quickies too. They can be just as much fun and can fit more easily into a busy couple's day.'

'Sex is one of the most satisfying forms of entertainment there is! Go with it, enjoy it, laugh, cry, love it!'

How do you rate your libido (on a scale of 1-5), 1 being very low, 5 being off the radar? Why do you think this is?

Happily most of you said 3-4.

'Varies. On the whole 3-4. I now appreciate the importance of sex and that being sexual isn't a bad thing. When I was younger, my libido was sometimes a 1.'

'4. Because I'm a very independent person, working many hours during the week for my own business. So when I have sex, I devote myself to it 110% like I have been starved from it (although that's not the case ☺).'

'I'll say 4 because my wife and I both enjoy sex and look forward to it on a regular basis. We're both still active in sports, which apparently boosts sex drive.'

'Probably a 3. Although I enjoy sex, I'm also shy about initiating it. Partly because I'm lazy and partly because I fear rejection from my partner who may be too tired to perform.'

'1. I'm now 68 and haven't had a regular sexual partner for a few months. I need to be "sparked off" by another person before I feel sexy.'

Do you think it's possible to maintain sexual desire in a long-term relationship?

'Yes I think it's possible, but it takes work. I think it comes down to trying new things and being able to laugh about the things that went horribly wrong. Once, my partner and I tried something during foreplay he had wanted to try before and I had tried with a previous partner. Turns out he felt weird about it afterwards, but we made it a joke and laughed about it. The laughter made us aware of how happy we are with each other, and thus we felt a need to be sexual together. Even though the experience itself wasn't good, we ended up more attracted to each other.'

'I like to think so. Changing things up has worked for us so far, different rooms, positions, places, props, etc.'

'Yes, it's possible. What has helped is (1) realising that sexual intimacy is important and making a point to engage in it regularly, and (2) being willing to trust each other and try new and exciting things in bed. What hasn't worked: relying on libido or romance to drive us to sex.'

'Yes. What works? Being aware of each other's moods and accepting that sometimes it's good to wait and that at other times it's good to "go with the flow". What doesn't work? Being insensitive.'

'We are in our 40s, have three kids and have been together for 12 years. We work long hours so it is difficult. Yes I think it's possible, but what has worked for us would not work for everyone but we do include sex with other people in our lives. Sometimes these people join us. Sometimes one of us has a 1-1 with someone else – usually my hubby. He has a small number of "fuck buddies" and also sees prostitutes. I am happy for him to do this but having 1-1s doesn't appeal to me. I think this can be full of danger and jealousy and swinging isn't for everyone. We have gone down this path cautiously with boundaries that suit us and give us the chance to safely explore and fulfill fantasies. It's something we do a few times a year not on a weekly basis. I also recommend making special day time for sex – i.e. taking time off work.'

'Yes, I do. We spice things up by going on dates and having "crazy sex time" when the kids are at school or on sleepovers. Crazy sex time is where we allow ourselves to get as loud and rambunctious as we like. The freedom to let loose really makes things more interesting. We're also not afraid to try new things.'

'Yes, it basically comes down to what the relationship is outside the bedroom. If you're with your best friend, and you treat each other as such, that level of emotional and physical trust translates into the bedroom. You never get tired of your best friend, and best friends confide, trust, test boundaries, explore new things, gain maturity, etc. Treat your lover and spouse as well as you treat your best friend.'

Do you have a positive body image? How does this impact on your relationships and sex life?

'It's becoming more positive and it impacts hugely. When I didn't feel good about my body I gave out the wrong vibes in terms of my availability, and it was only when I realised that you don't have to have long legs and be gorgeous to be sexy, that I realised my body was alright. My sex life has improved accordingly!'

'What woman does? But, it doesn't affect my sex life or relationship because my man likes what he sees and is not afraid to remind me. It makes me comfortable with him, even though I would like to trim a few inches here and there.'

'Yes, maybe if I didn't I'd be ashamed of someone seeing my love handles. If you're reluctant to toss off your clothes, your sex life can't be that great.'

'Yes, absolutely. I was a dancer. More comfortable with other dancers or pudgy, middle-aged scientists who are smarter than I am. Two of the best lovers I've had were a principal dancer with the Royal Ballet, and chief of a pathology department at the University of California, San Francisco.'

'We are both happy with our bodies and yes we are both a bit saggy, flabby and overweight. I am about 21lbs more than I should be. I think we could have a better sex life if we were thinner and fitter. Just for better stamina and trying new positions.'

'For the most part I think I do. The most important part is that my partner loves my body unconditionally and that makes me feel much more positive and more open to being naked for prolonged amounts of time, which always helps.'

'I am chubby, but I love my body. It's not what your body looks like, but what you do with the body you have.'

Help List

Sexual Health

Family Planning Association (FPA)

50 Featherstone Street, London EC1Y 8QU
www.fpa.org.uk
Prioritises sexual health as a public health issue in the UK. Runs campaigns to improve sexual health services and holds talks, workshops and training courses for health-care professionals and consumers. Sexual health clinic finder and advice line (Tel: 0845 122 8690).

NetDoctor

c/o Natmags, 33 Broadwick Street, London W1F 9EP
www.netdoctor.co.uk
NetDoctor is an independent website collaboration between doctors, health-care professionals, information specialists and patients, providing advice on male and female sexual health and contraception.

NHS Direct

120 Leman Street, London E1 8EU
Tel: 0845 4647 (helpline)
www.nhsdirect.nhs.uk
NHS Direct provides help and advice on a range of topics including male and female sexual health and contraception.

Counselling services

Relate

Premier House, Carolina Court, Lakeside, Doncaster, DN4 5RA.
Tel: 0300 100 1234
www.relate.org.uk
Provides relationship counselling, sex therapy, workshops and training courses for individuals and couples.

The Tavistock Centre for Couple Relationships

70 Warren Street, London W1T 5PB
Tel: 0207 380 1960
www.tccr.org.uk
Provides a range of relationship, psychosexual counselling and parenting support services in London. Also holds talks and workshops on various aspects of sex and relationships in association with *Psychologies* magazine.

Sex coaching

Dr Lisa Turner

www.the-o-coach.com
www.energytransmutation.com
Dr Lisa Turner is the founder of Psycademy coach training and runs online courses in energy transmutation for increased intimacy, better sex and more fulfilling relationships.

Dr Tara Few

www.uksexcoach.com
Dr Tara Few is a sex coach based in Cambridge. Her work helps people to find their own sexual style and to take action to gain the life they want.

Rachel Foux

www.rachelfoux.com
Rachel Foux is a sex and relationship coach based in London/Herts. She specialises in sex and relationships in pregnancy and the early parenting years. She is dedicated to enabling people to enhance and enrich the ways they deal with personal issues to discover fulfillment in love, life and relationships.

Uta Demontis

www.manawa.co.uk
Sex and relationship coach specialising in Taoist sexual health practices. Runs jade love egg workshops at Coco de Mer

Vena Ramphal

www.venaramphal.com
Vena Ramphal is a London-based passion coach whose work draws on the classical Indian energy traditions: yoga, tantra and kama sutra. She works with those in relationship flux and can help people to cultivate a deeper experience of erotic pleasure.

Sex-positive education and events

BDSM/Fetish

Bisexuality

www.bisexualindex.org.uk
Bisexual Resource Center (US-based) offers support and community links for bisexuals. Links to the UK Bi-scene.

The Body Electric School

www.b-e-school.com
Helping people to explore their potential as fully integrated, loving and self-aware beings through personal growth experiences, touch, massage and conscious breathing courses.

Erotic massage

The New School of Erotic Touch
www.eroticmassage.com
A learning community of pleasure activists providing online education DVDs and articles about the healing art of touch.

Kinky Salon

www.kinkysalonlondon.co.uk
A worldwide community dedicated to safe, consensual and playful artistic and erotic self-expression. They run volunteer-based events in London.

The London Fetish Fair (Sunday market)

Shillibeers, Carpenter's Mews (next to the Pleasance Theatre), North Road, Islington, N7 9EF.
www.londonfetishfair.co.uk
Cabaret, fashion, after party, and educational workshops in all aspects of fetish and BDSM.

The London School of Mistressing

www.londonschoolofmistressing.com
Baker Street tube/Marylebone Chambers.
Mistress Josephine runs courses for individuals and couples looking to explore fetish and power play within a relationship. She also offers training in how to set up as a mistress.

Planet Midori

www.planetmidori.com
www.fhp-inc.com (classes and workshops)
Sex educator and columnist on adventurous sexuality. Author of *The Seductive Art of Japanese Bondage* and *Wild Side Sex: The Book of Kink*. She offers humorous classes to help people spice up their sex lives and encouraging self-discovery and personal growth.

Polyamory

www.polyamory.org
Explores all types of polyamory and bisexuality. News group, mailing list.

Sacred Pleasures

The Pot, Hackney Wick, London
Tel: 07583 343 928
www.sacredkink.co.uk
Concious sexuality workshops – BDSM and tantra for personal growth and pleasure. London Faerie offers conscious BDSM for pleasure and personal growth, kinky coaching and initiation, Bondassage full body sensual BDSM, and shadow healing for energy release. He works with intuition, energy release and intention to create a magical space, helping you to grow, move forward and feel fantastically sexy en route!

Tantra

Rebecca Lowrie (London)

www.rebeccalowrie.com
Sacred sexual expansion and exploration. Private sessions and workshops for individuals and couples exploring sacred, conscious sexuality, intimacy, sensuality and more. info@rebeccalowrie.com, 07903 014 364.

Shakti Tantra: An Invitation to Pleasure (South West)

www.shaktitantra.co.uk
School of sexuality and tantra run by Hilly Spenceley and Sue Newsome.

The Tantric Path (John Hawken)

The Field of Dreams, Sancreed, Penzance, TR20 8QX
www.thetantricpath.com
Weekend beginner courses, advanced courses on issues around sexuality,
freedom and pleasure, and a one-year transformational tantric training course.

Tantralink (London and Herts)

www.sensual-soirees.com – parties with heart – music, tantra games, dance,
massage, food and connections.

Taoism

London Universal Healing Tao Centre

1st Floor, 68 Great Eastern Street, London EC2A 3JT
www.healing-tao.co.uk
Learning and teaching the Taoist arts based on the work of Mantak Chia. Nine-step
Taoist training in meditational, martial, self-development, healing, and tantric and
shamanic aspects of Taoist practice.

Sex and relationship courses and information

The Institute for the Advanced Study of Human Sexuality

www.wlx.com/ysilva/iashs
Provides study programmes in sexuality and has the largest resource library in
the world.

The Kinsey Institute for Research in Sex, Gender and Reproduction

www.kinseyinstitute.org
Interdisciplinary research in the field of human sexuality and related aspects of
gender reproduction.

Loveology University

www.loveologyuniversity.com
Online sex and relationship courses by sexologist Dr Ava Cadell.

The Society for Human Sexuality

www.sexuality.org
An online resource for sex and relationship information from Washington University, USA

Vulva University

www.houseochicks.com
Providing award-winning (and excellent value!) online classes. Intelligent and thoughtful information taught by sex educators, college professors and published authors. Founded in 1996 by Dorrie Lane.

Sex personals

www.adultfriendfinder.com – UK's largest swinging site.
www.fetlife.com – free social networking for BDSM/fetish events nationwide.
www.polymatchmaker.com – for polyamorists.
www.sensual-spirit.com – dating and social network for singles, couples, polyamorists and beyond.

Erotic boutiques

Bordello

www.bordello-london.com
Designer lingerie, sex books, toys and educational workshops in burlesque, making your own luxury lingerie, nipple tassels, and millinery.

Coco de Mer

23 Monmouth Street, Covent Garden, London
www.coco-de-mer.com
Luxury erotic boutique with education as its ethos.

Jo Divine

www.jodivine.com
A UK-based store selling skin-safe luxury sex toys, vibrators, and dildos.

Organic Pleasures

Tel: 0131 6220636
www.organicpleasures.co.uk
Edinburgh-based erotic boutique developing its own branded organic product range.

She Said Erotic Boutique

11Ship Street Gardens, Brighton, BN1 1AJ
www.shesaidboutique.com
Lingerie, corsets, bridalwear, boudoir, adult toys and erotic art, salons and workshops.

Sh! Womenstore

57 Hoxton Square, London N1 6HD
www.sh-womenstore.com
Women's erotic boutique with education classes.

Erotic book publishers

Erotic Artists

Association of Erotic Artists
3/50 Britannia Street, London WC1X 9JH
www.associationoferoticartists.co.uk
Campaigning for the erotic arts and artists working within the genre. Art, photography books, erotic literature and DVDs, articles and essays.

Erotic Readers and Writers Association

www.erotica-readers.com
International community of men and women interested in the erotic/sensual.
Original erotic fiction, sexy toy and adult movie recommendations, plus a forum
'Inside the Erotic Mind' decicated to adult issues, activities and relationships.

Magazines

The Erotic Review

www.eroticreviewmagazine.com
A lively, intelligent approach to erotica and sex appealing to our primary sex
organ – the brain! Fiction, features, photos, art portfolios, books, theatre, sex
toys and guides.

Loving More

www.lovemore.com
Educational website, magazine and online poly community.

Psychologies

www.psychologies.co.uk
Women's magazine for life-curious women that helps you to grow more,
know more. Covers the self, relationships, family, work, beauty and wellbeing,
culture, travel and more.

Skin Two

BCM Box 2071, London, WC1N 3XX
www.skintwo.co.uk
Fetish/BDSM clubs, parties, fashion, art, photography and all things kinky.
Organises the annual Skin Two Rubber Ball.

Body piercing

European Professional Piercers' Association (EPPA)

www.eapp.eu

Tattoos

Tattoo Club of Great Britain

www.tattoo.co.uk
Alliance of Professional Tattooists
A non-profit educational organisation founded in 1992 to address health and safety issues facing the tattoo industry. Features a worldwide members list.
www.safe-tattoos.com

National conferences, balls and exhibitions

Erotica UK

www.eroticauk.com
The UK's biggest erotic lifestyle exhibition and Winter Ball (takes place every November at London Olympia).

The Night of the Senses Ball

www.erotic-awards.co.uk
Annual charity ball founded by Tuppy Owens, which raises funds for the Outsiders Trust, which helps disabled people find sexual partners. Begins with the Erotic Awards presentation and show, stage acts, female wrestling and cabaret acts.

Female-friendly porn filmmakers

Anna Span

www.annaspansdiary.com
Anna is the author of *Shoot Your Own Adult Home Movies*.

Candida Royalle

www.candidaroyalle.com
American producer and director of couples' porn via her company Femme Productions. Author of *How to Tell a Naked Man What to do*.

Erika Lust

www.erikalust.com
Filmmaker, writer and founder of Lust Films of Barcelona. Erika has directed several award-winning adult films and also sells erotic books and magazines. She has a feminine, aesthetic and innovative approach to porn and aims to excite your mind.

Petra Joy

www.petrajoy.com
Brighton-based sex-positive erotic filmmaker, photographer and journalist. Her work is a visual journey into erotic female fantasies, which she describes as 'art core' rather than hardcore.

Cookery holidays for couples

www.cookinfrance.com

A top cookery school in France run by celebrity chef Jim Fisher and his wife Lucy. They offer a range of cookery classes including *Cooking as Foreplay - Beyond Aphrodisiacs*, which is designed for lovers of all ages.

Glossary

Age-play
A form of role-play that involves pretending to be younger (or older) than you are, e.g. teacher/student.

Analingus (rimming)
Oral stimulation of the anus externally or internally, using a dental dam for protection against STIs.

Anal sex (sodomy)
Inserting a penis into the anus, or using a strap-on, for sexual pleasure.

Aphrodisiac
A substance that increases or enhances sexual desire.

Bartholin's glands
Two small glands around the entrance of the vagina that secrete fluid when a woman is sexually aroused.

Bastinado
Foot whipping with a cane or flogger.

BDSM
A catch-all term for bondage and discipline, dominance and submission, and sadism and masochism.

Ben wa balls
Small metal balls that are worn inside the vagina for sexual stimulation.

Body modification
Altering the body for ritualistic or spiritual purposes or to signify a sub/dom relationship, e.g. tattooing, piercing, scarification, and branding.

Bondage
Restraining someone with rope/cuffs/tape/scarves for consensual sexual pleasure.

Breath-play (asphyxiaphilia)
Restricting a submissive's oxygen flow with a bondage mask to create an orgasmic high. Advanced play that can be dangerous.

Butt plug
A flared sex toy that is inserted into the anus during sex or masturbation. It is held in place by the sphincter muscles.

Chastity devices
Sex toys for restraining the penis, testicles and vagina for erotic pain/pleasure.

Clitoris
A small bud at the top of the labia, which gives a woman intense sexual pleasure. The hood is visible externally and the crura (clitoral wings) extend like a wishbone inside the body. Vaginal orgasms are therefore clitoral in origin.

Cock and ball training (CBT) or 'ball play'
Manipulating the scrotum and testicles for erotic pleasure e.g. chastity devices for bondage, stretching, and slapping.

Cock ring
A rubber or metal band that is worn at the base of the penis to trap blood flow enabling a man to stay erect for longer.

Cowper's glands
Two small glands found beneath the prostate gland that produce part of the seminal fluid.

Cunnilingus
Using your mouth, lips and tongue on the vulva and vagina, to give a woman sexual pleasure. The term is Latin for 'cunnus' – vulva and 'lingus' – to lick.

Cupping therapy
A form of alternative medicine using medical cups on the skin to stimulate blood flow and healing. Fire is used to heat the rim to create a temporary seal and suction on the skin. It feels pleasurable on the breasts and genitals and can be used to mark the skin temporarily for ritual play.

Dental dam
A sterile latex square used for oral sex and rimming; protects against STIs and E.coli.

116

Dildo
Rubber, silicone or latex sex toy for vaginal or anal penetration. Dildos come in various shapes and sizes.

Dyspareunia
A medical term for painful sex.

Edgeplay
Using a scene to push your lover to his or her physical and psychological limits for personal growth and sexual expansion. Also refers to BDSM activities that are deemed 'edgy' such as fire-play, knife-play or erotic asphyxiation, and the tantric practice of learning how to separate orgasm and ejaculation to build sexual energy.

Ejaculation
Rhythmic, pleasurable contractions that propel semen out of the penis during orgasm.

Electro stimulation (Electro sex)
Using electrical devices for sexual pleasure, most commonly TENS machines and Violet Wands. Advanced BDSM play that needs to be taught.

Endorphins
Chemicals produced by the body to help us deal with stress and pain. They make us feel temporarily high. Exercise, sex and BDSM play scenes all create endorphins.

Enema (colonics)
Cleansing the bowel for health and erotic purposes, as a precursor to anal play or rimming. You can buy home enema kits online.

Erogenous zones
Areas of the body that are sensitive to touch and can arouse desire.

Exhibitionism
Having sex or exposing your genitals in a public setting for sexual pleasure.

Fellatio (blow job)
Using your mouth, lips and tongue on a man's penis to give him sexual pleasure.

Fetish

An object, body part or piece of clothing that heightens sexual fantasy. Leather, rubber, footwear, body parts or silk/soft materials are common fetishes. 'Partialism' is being aroused by a particular body part such as feet.

Fetters

Foot restraints.

Fisting (handballing)

Slowly inserting the hand into the vagina or anus for sexual pleasure.

Flagellation

Flogging, whipping, spanking or paddling a lover methodically to explore the pain/pleasure link. Can be done with canes, whips, paddles, rulers, belts or floggers.

Frottage

Rubbing against someone's body for sexual pleasure.

Gender-play

A play scene that involves pretending to be the opposite sex as power exchange for pleasure.

Golden shower (watersports)

Urinating on your lover or vice versa, for erotic pleasure.

G-spot

Erectile tissue on the anterior vaginal wall, which may feel pleasurable when stimulated. Named after German gynaecologist Ernst Grafenberg.

Gonzo porn

Amateur or 'no frills' porn, which uses a handheld camera to place the viewer in the scene. Close-ups are filmed in a disjointed style similar to the writing style of 'gonzo journalism'. Started by John Stagliano and the popular Buttman.com films.

Insertables

A term for vibrators, toys that are used internally to stimulate the nerves for sexual pleasure.

Kegel (PC) exercises

Resistance and release exercises using a love egg/vaginal toner to strengthen the pelvic muscles and improve sensation and orgasm. Developed by Dr Arnold Kegel.

Leather

A common fetish. 'Leatherfolk' refers to the S/M community, which originated in the US.

Love egg

An egg-shaped vibrator or stone used vaginally to tone and stimulate the vagina and pelvic muscles. Jade love eggs can be worn during the day and are good for pelvic toning and strengthening orgasms.

Lubricant

A liquid that reduces friction and makes penetration easier, enhancing sexual pleasure. Lubes come in various types – water-based, silicone-based and oil-based.

Master (top/dominant)

A person who takes control of a play scene or sexual lifestyle.

Mummification

Using layers or equipment to immobilise a submissive/bottom during a play scene.

Ménage à trois

A 'household of three' lovers at once...

Munch

A social gathering for those interested in exploring BDSM. They take place in local pubs/restaurants and there's no formal dress code. FetLife lists local munches around the UK.

Orgasm

The peak of sexual pleasure and excitement, which causes rhythmic contractions in the vagina and penis. A multiple orgasm is when a woman has several sequential contractions, which can get stronger.

Pegging

Penetrating the anus with a strap-on dildo.

Perineum

The patch of skin between the vulva or scrotum and anus. It is often sensitive and responsive to massage.

Pervertibles

A term coined by leather activist David Stein to describe non-sexual objects that can used for sexual purposes, e.g. pegs, rulers, candles, an electric toothbrush etc.

Play party

An organised event that typically involves an education workshop about an aspect of BDSM followed by a play party to practise skills learnt.

Play piercing (needle play)

Using sterile needles to pierce the skin for ritual purposes, sexual expression and growth. Creates an endorphin high. Needs to be done by a trained person.

Pornography

Sexually-stimulating written or visual works. Comes from the Greek word 'porneia' which translates as 'the writings of and about prostitutes'.

Pre-ejaculate (pre-cum)

Fluid secreted by the Cowper's glands that is secreted through the tip of the penis during arousal before a man ejaculates. It's why the withdrawal method is not considered to be safe sex.

Pro-Domme (dominatrix)

A woman who offers BDSM services (not always sexual) for money.

Prostate gland

A walnut/dome shaped gland around 3cm inside a man's anus. It secretes a fluid that makes up semen and assists in the ejaculation process. It's called the 'male G-spot' because it can induce pleasure and orgasms and brings on the urge to pee!

P-spot (prostate) play

A form of anal play using a specially designed toy, or finger, to stimulate the male prostate internally and keep it healthy. Can be stimulated externally by massaging the area between the anus and scrotum.

Refractory period

A stage in the sexual response cycle after orgasm when a man is no longer able to get an erection. It can last for minutes, hours or days depending on his age.

Sadomasochism (S/M)

Getting pleasure from sexual acts in which you inflict or receive erotic pain or humiliation. Sadism is named after the French aristocrat Marquis de Sade who was imprisoned for sexual domination. Masochism is named after the Austrian writer Leopold von Sacher-Masoch, who wrote about his desires to be dominated by Venus in Furs.

Safety scissors

Bondage or surgical scissors that enable you to cut through rope quickly.

Safe word

A special term to stop a play scene immediately. The traffic light system is common – 'red' for stop, 'green' for play, and 'yellow' for slow down.

Scene

Refers to sex play between a top/bottom (dominant and submissive). A chance to explore fantasies within a defined time limit with someone you trust.

Semen

A white, milky fluid secreted by the penis when a man ejaculates. It contains 'sperm' which are reproductive cells.

Sensate focus exercises

Sex therapy exercises that encourage couples to explore sensual arousal without penetration to increase sensual awareness and reduce performance anxiety.

Sexually transmitted infections (STIs)

A bacterial or viral infection that is passed on via unprotected anal, oral or vaginal sex.

Shibari

Beautiful and decorative Japanese-style rope bondage.

Skene's gland

The 'female prostate', tiny glands on the vulva that produce lubricant and ejaculate during arousal.

Strap-on
A dildo and harness used for sex play between women or for anal play between a man and a woman.

Submissive (bottom/boy)
Someone who prefers to be dominated during a scene. The art of letting go into ecstasy.

Tantra
Eastern spiritual and sexual practices that increase sensuality and intimacy. Tantra is Sanskrit for 'woven together'.

Vaginismus
A spasm of the muscles around that vagina that makes intercourse painful and difficult. Caused by a combination of physical and psychological factors and can be treated with sex therapy.

Vanilla sex
Missionary sex between a man and woman that doesn't involve kink play.

Vibrators
Sex toys that can be used by men and women to enhance pleasure and orgasm. They come in all shapes and sizes and common types include the Rabbit, butterfly vibe, clitoral vibe, G-spot and bullet vibe.

Vulvodynia
A stinging, painful or burning sensation in the vulva, which can be treated.

Wartenburg wheel
A medical device made of stainless steel that was designed for neurological use. It has sharp pins that are rolled across the skin to stimulate the nerves. A popular sex toy to create erotic pain of varying intensity.

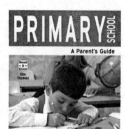
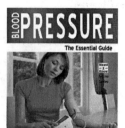